D0061536

Autism and the God Connection

Redefining the Autistic Experience through
Extraordinary Accounts of Spiritual Giftedness

William Stillman

SOURCEBOOKS, INC.
NAPERVILLE, ILLINOIS

Published by Sourcebooks, Inc.
P.O. Box 4410, Naperville, Illinois 60567-4410
(630) 961-3900
FAX: (630) 961-2168
www.sourcebooks.com

Library of Congress Cataloging-in-Publication Data
Stillman, William
  Autism and the God connection / William Stillman.
    p. cm.
Includes bibliographical references.
ISBN-13: 978-1-4022-0649-8
ISBN-10: 1-4022-0649-6
1. Autism. 2. Autism in children. 3. Autism--Religious aspects. I. Title.

RJ506.A9S75 2006
616.85'882--dc22
                                        2005031354

Printed and bound in the United States of America.
VP 10 9 8 7 6 5 4 3 2 1

Praise for *Autism and the God Connection*

"This book is a must-read, whether you love someone with an autistic-spectrum disorder, or work in the field. William Stillman describes a parallel process of discovering his own spirituality, while exploring the heightened spiritual connectedness of those he works with. The result provides a deep sense of hope and understanding that I've not experienced with other books on autistic-spectrum disorders."
—Jeffrey A. Naser, MD, Medical Director, Main Line Clinical Associates

"Thank you, William Stillman, for confirming what I have suspected to be true—our son is a gift with a special mission to fulfill on the planet earth. The stories in your life-affirming book show us that parents of children on the autism spectrum have been blessed with an opportunity for greater spiritual meaning in their lives. *Autism and the God Connection* will transform the way our society views 'so called' disabilities."
—Nancy Alspaugh, author of *Not Your Mother's Midlife* and *Fearless Women: Midlife Portraits*, and mother of ASD child.

"I had often wondered if there were many others with autism who have spiritual experiences similar to mine, so I appreciated Stillman's courage in writing this revealing book. While many without autism also develop spiritual gifts, it is important that people recognize this in those with autism, so I highly recommend *Autism and the God Connection*. I believe we live in an age of spiritual awakening and Stillman's research is a great example of this."
—Penelope McMullen, Catholic Sister, person with autism, and author of "The Gifted Side of Autism," *Focus on Autism and Other Developmental Disabilities*

"Speaking from the heart, William Stillman provides us with a unique look at autism's inner soul. This wonderful book should be required reading for parents of special children, and especially for teachers and clinicians who may be making some incorrect assumptions about the inner vitality and intellectual abilities of autistic function. Definitely an illuminating and inspiring read!"
—Dorita S. Berger, author of *Music Therapy, Sensory Integration and the Autistic Child*

"The information and descriptions noted about the autistic experience in *Autism and the God Connection* should be well received by those touched with autism and by the understanding people who know them. It is like a breath of fresh air, a release of knowledge and feelings that were avoided and rarely acknowledged as truth. The accumulation and presentation of this information should enlighten people in the field of autism as well as people who want to help people.

We all need to take a fresh look at who we are and who the individuals are that we are trying to help. We need to realize their attributes, promote the recognition and development of such, and enjoy the beauty of each individual as one of God's creations. Mr Stillman takes us to a new dimension of understanding of self and others; but understanding with which we should become better acquainted and of which we should make better use."
—William L. Jones, Ed.D., Faculty Emeritus, Dept. of Special Ed., Bloomsburg University

"An intensely rare and innovative book! William Stillman has opened the door to a most intriguing partnership between the treatment of autism and metaphysical studies. The personal stories of autistics as narrated in this book parallel the "multisensory" experiences described by intuitives, mystics, and psychics and call to mind the abilities of shaman who are able to traverse between the world of spirit and this physical plane. What an amazing realization that those long considered mentally challenged may actually be far more advanced in terms of *spiritual* perception, and it is we who must strive to advance to their level of understanding."
—Kathy L. Callahan, PhD, author of *Multisensory Human: The Evolution of the Soul*

For Frank and Nora—

To whom I am forever indebted

And to all those who demonstrated their belief and support
by contributing to this volume, I thank you.

Contents

Preface

⌘

A human being is part of the whole called the "universe," a part limited in time and space. He experiences himself, his thoughts, and feelings as something separated from the rest, a kind of optical delusion...of consciousness. This delusion is a kind of prison for us, restricting us to our personal desires and to affection for a few persons nearest to us. Our task must be to free ourselves from this prison by widening our circle of compassion to embrace all living creatures and the whole of nature in all its beauty. Nobody is able to achieve this completely, but the striving for such achievement is in itself part of the liberation and a foundation for inner security.

—Albert Einstein

Acknowledgments

Foremost, I thank God, the Creator and author of the Universe, for all the blessings and privileges of my truly extraordinary life.

Some of the individuals who contributed to this book did so under the condition of anonymity. Still others I elected to protect under the guise of pseudonyms or on a first-name basis only. My grateful thanks to those who unconditionally supported my moving forward in telling the truth. I have learned volumes under your gracious tutorship; please accept this book as my valentine to you all. Among the friends, allies, and associates I can adore by name, I count:

Joseph Allen, Pat Amos, Larry Anderson, Debra J. Andreas, Dr. Janiece Andrews, P.M.H. Atwater, Dr. Linnea Bailey, David Baldner, Dr. Beth Barol, John Baron, John and Sue Baron, Sr., Barbara Benitez, Joan Berquist, Clint Billotte, Janet Billotte, Andrew Bloomfield, Elizabeth Bloomfield, Ursula Bowler, Kathy Brant, Ann Brennan, Larry Brody, Cindy Buckley, Holly Burke, Jon Burns, Joannie Busillo-Aguayo, Charles Byrd, Mary Nell Byrd, Christian Ciaramella, Corey Patrick Cavanaugh, Dennis, Colleen,

Brendon and Kylie Cavanaugh, Jasmine L. Chandra, Carol Chastain, Renee Chastain, Eric Chessen, Sabina Childers, Daniel Colvin, James Comisar, Alex "Clay" Cotto, Mary Ellen Crawford, Patrick Davis, William Davis, Heather Dawson, Galen Deck, Jason Delecki, Rick Dieffenbaugher, Sarah Donten, Lea Ann Driscoll, Dennis Duscha, Lois Duscha, Kenneth Ealey, Matthew Efaw, Jeremiah Evans, Avery Ezzi, Leslie Ezzi, Preston Freemer, Ricky Fox, Nicki Fischer, Tina Franquet, Leigh Ann Fulford, Sharon Rose Gabet, Dan and Toni Gage, Sissi Garvey, Carol Gilligan, Emily Gilligan, Gail Gillingham, Gregory Ginoble, Richard Glosser, Donelle Gonzalez, Nathan Grant, Angela Greenwood, Susan Greenwood, Timothy Griffin, Cindy Gwinn, Mary Ann Harrington, Mary Jo Harris, Joseph Harrold, Kay Haun, Brandon Henken, Kristine Henley, Linda Henry, Brian Henson, Kenneth Hoffman, Susan Howell, Holly Hricko, Michael Hricko, Eric Jones, Caryn Kadel, Amy Kenevan, Kathy Kenevan, Melanie Ketchem, Robin Ketchem, Chris Khumprakob, Fran Kilgore, Dr. Moya Kinnealey, Lori Klein, Pastor David M. Klinedinst, Annabelle Klinger, John and Shawn Klorzyck, Zack Klorzyck, Herbert Knapp, Martin Knight, Claire Komacek, Debra Kranzel, Isadore Kranzel, Rosalyn Kranzel, Marlene Kubina, Renee Labbie, Jeffrey Ladd, Mary Lapos, Dianne Lasher, Tucker Lautt, Debbie Leggens, Scott Leggens, Joe and Ginny Leonard, Matthew Leonard, Devlyn Lighthawk, Christine Little, Beth Ann Lynn, Earl Lynn, Cassidy Maddas, John and Jennifer Maddas, Chris and Kari Main, Katelyn Main, Bradley Mains, Thomas Magill, Stuart Marshall, Janette Martin, John Henry Meyer, J.R. Miller, Kathy Miller,

Sharon Mavko, Rosa McAllister, Logan McCoy, Shane and Patty McCoy, Fred and Patti McPoyle, Maria Nagy Medved, Jennifer Messinger, Larry Miller, Barbara Moran, Isabelle Mosca, Angela Murphy, James Murphy, Sharon Muzio, Jamie O'Neill, Julia Novak, Teri Pacion, Reverend Ziek Paterniti, Ashley Pennington, Teri Pentz, Mary Pritchard, Daniel Rader, Roia Rafieyan, Alisha Raiford-Hall, Delores Ramie, Heidi Reichenbach, Ann Reeves, Mark Reeves, David Rider, Robin Rice, Hector Rivera, Dr. Jessica W. Rivers, Nancy Richey, Sherri Rizzo, Sharon Rose, Carroll Rottmund, Lori Rottmund, Mark Sachnik, Helen Sanders, Aaron Scaccia, Jay Scarfone, Kathy, Jason and Alex Scarfone, Bonnie Schaefer, Scott Schultz, Joanne Schruers, Neal Schwarzchild, Barbara Scott-Mazza, Johnny Seitz, Paula Sessing, Jennifer Seybert, Kendall Seybert, Daniel Shallenberger, Dayna Shallenberger, Shannon Shaull, Stephen Shore, Rich Shull, Betty Silagyi, Teresa Smollinger, John Spina, Barbara Sprouls, Jason Sprouls, Beulah Stillman, Donna Szamatowicz, Nancy Thomas, Leslie Thompson, Jennifer Thompson, Julean Thorpe, Nicole Todd, Amy Townsley, Will Turnbull, Frank and Rae Unger, Mary Vickers, Ryan Walters, Ambry Ward, Frank Ward, Jr., Adam Weber, Ann, Mike and Emily Weber, Matthew Weigand, Dee Welker, Cindy Wenger, Birgit Werth, Fred Werth, Carl Whitmore, Tom Wink, Deirdre Wright, Sarah Wright, and Michael Zack.

I am grateful to Dr. William Jones, Dr. Kristie Koenig, Cynthia Sue Larson, and Patrice Smedley for their comments about my manuscript which confirmed my intentions and assured me that I was doing what was right and true and good and kind.

Donna Williams, author of *Nobody Nowhere*, deserves select acknowledgment for her candor and for conceding that, in composing this book, my heart is in the right place.

Special thanks to Rachel Simon, author of *Riding the Bus with My Sister*, for making time to review an early draft of my manuscript and offering her astute and invaluable professional insights.

My deepest appreciation to Bethany Brown, my editor at Sourcebooks, for "getting it" from the get-go and championing my cause from the start.

Finally, but far from least, profound gratitude, love, and blessings to my agent, June Clark, whose belief in me and the importance of what I have to offer never for a moment faltered.

Introduction

❧

If you're about to begin reading this book, you may be one of the 71 percent of Americans who, according to a 2003 poll, is interested in learning more about autism. You've likely seen or heard the almost-daily news reports that reference or headline the subject. Maybe someone you know has a child with autism—a friend, a coworker, a relation, yourself. If the title caught your attention, you might be curious to learn about autism and a strong spiritual connection; perhaps you've already experienced firsthand this divine association. Or are you simply open-minded enough to want to know more about autism from a completely unique perspective? I know I was. But absorbing it all was an unexpected journey, the path of which led to professional and personal revelations.

To those unfamiliar with autism, it is, from a clinical perspective, a neurological difference in how the brain is "wired." There is no single known cause, though theories abound and current research is focused upon genetic and environmental factors. (As recently as 1997, a nursing text-book was proffering the ancient stereotype that indifferent, "refrigerator" mothers were accountable for their children's

2 ◡ Autism and the God Connection

autistic disassociation!) Autism primarily affects one's ability to communicate in ways that are effective, reliable, and universally understandable. This means many folks do not speak, or they have limited vocal capacity. These obstacles impede one's expressions of wants, needs, thoughts, and desires. This cannot help but impact the quality of one's social interactions. The challenge to sustain social relationships is another hallmark of autistic diagnosis.

Autism is also diagnosed by marked differences in fine and gross motor skills. These may include repetitive activities such as physically rocking back and forth, twirling a piece of string, flicking a light switch on and off repeatedly, or simply lacking in grace and agility of movement. (Some with autism have complained that certain physical traits are not of their volition, akin to a prolonged, involuntary shiver, sneeze, or twitch.)

Autism is a lifelong experience, and is neither contagious nor curable. It is, quite simply, a natural part of someone's being, every bit as much as eye or hair color, flesh pigmentation, and ancestral heritage—as unique and individual as each individual is unique. It manifests on a broad, multicolored spectrum that stretches from those who "appear" to be significantly challenged to those with very mild experiences. For example, I identify closely with Asperger's Syndrome especially in reflection of my childhood, adolescence, and young adulthood. Asperger's is presently defined as one of autism's "cousins" on that broad spectrum. It is considered a milder, high-functioning form of that experience, and I am able to commiserate comfortably with others so identified.

ALL THAT I AM

For me, Asperger's has meant a lifelong inability to interpret many social conventions and interactions, including humor and subtleties of innuendo in conversation. Instead, my interpretation is often very literal and concrete. At times it is like a real-life rendition of Abbott and Costello's "Who's on First?"

> *Hotel front desk clerk upon check-in:*
> "I hope you'll enjoy your stay, Mr. Stillman.
> Your room is right down the hall from me."
>
> *Stillman (incredulous):*
> "You mean you're staying here too?"

Asperger's has also meant my favoring topics of personal passion over relationships with people. "People" was a foreign language, and like many a tourist, one that I could employ just well enough to pass. (Example: Note to self—remarking after someone brings you a glass of H_2O, "You make good water!" almost always gets a laugh or smile.) As a result, I was often overlooked, maligned, or disregarded by others and still am to some extent.

Finally, like my brothers and sisters with autism, my entire *nervous system* is intensely sensitive such that my emotions and senses "vibrate" at a frequency different than most. For instance, I was unusually sensitive as a child—extremely emotional. The melancholy lyrics to a song like "Puff the Magic Dragon" or virtually anything by Peter, Paul and Mary could cause me to become inconsolable. This was, perhaps, most memorably defined by an emancipating childhood incident.

Raised in the Episcopal church, I was once removed from my pew, at age six, because I could not control my weeping. Unbeknownst to anyone, I had been staring at a terrible, glorious stained-glass window of the crucifixion and grieving for the pain Christ must have endured. The arresting mosaic of that forlorn image etched itself indelibly upon me. And yet at some point, I became emotionally and empathically detached.

As a small boy, I often experienced the sensation of déjà vu. It manifested in a sudden realization that what was occurring in the moment had already been experienced exactly the same way once before. I also used to see things move out of the corner of my eye, or have prophetic dreams like the one in which I picked countless pennies up off our front lawn and, the next day in reality, did just that—wondering how on earth the coins got there to begin with. But then my family was always of the thinking that was open to unexplainable possibilities and events.

I cannot remember a time when I wasn't completely enraptured by the fantasy of *The Wizard of Oz*, and it became my foremost passion. Other childhood "sub-passions" tended toward unusual or mystic themes that held future portent. These included a fascination with gargoyles on churches and cathedrals; Greek mythology, especially Perseus and Medusa; purported "real life" monsters including Bigfoot, extraterrestrials, and the Loch Ness Monster; and Wonder Woman, from the popular 1970s television series. Unlike most teenagers of my era, I was completely disinterested in *Star Wars*, being, instead, drawn to the realism of *Close Encounters of the Third Kind*. I was also intrigued by stories of ghosts and what was then called "the occult." Complicating matters was that *nowhere* in my readings of unusual phenomena such as ESP was spirituality or a benevolent Creator referenced as the foundation for any of it. This reinforced my rigid belief that any such "powers" were of impure origins.

I have always felt that something or *someone* was watching over me, offering protection where warranted. I say "where warranted" because I certainly haven't been immune to every harmful or distressing circumstance in my life; and beginning at a young age I endured daily humiliations of varied forms—verbal and physical—from my peers because I was different. This abuse persisted through much of my school career. I now know that to have been "rescued" from those experiences would have diverted the process necessary for me to learn and grow from them. Ultimately, it made me strong. But with my own sense of self quickly eroding then, I was unable to discern such learning opportunities through the strife and muck. As I descended into this murky period, any spiritual connection was impeded, and I rejected precisely what was protecting me.

In retrospect, there was a pattern of perpetual struggle between a "light," good, or spiritual side and a "dark," menacing side that feeds from self-loathing. Fortunately, I've always relied upon an innate sense of purpose in life, a pre-destiny for recognition of what I had to offer the world. Something inside told me that if I could ride out the rough times things would improve, somehow, someway. Contemplating a straight razor in my darkest hour, it was that inner protective voice which prevented me from taking my own life at sixteen. It is crucial to note that it is not unusual for many young adults with autism or Asperger's to reach this dark place and entertain suicidal ideations. Others numb their pain and self-medicate using drugs, nicotine, and alcohol. Parents and caregivers must be especially vigilant in observing any symptoms of depression and post-traumatic stress disorder. A strong spiritual foundation may well be a resource to those struggling through such times, but by the time I had reached that point I was virtually disconnected. This played out over the course of my young life and well into adulthood until I consciously aligned with an authentic source. It evolved into the light side emerging exalted and victorious. I credit those with autism for providing the nourishment that was my impetus, as you will learn.

SPIRITUALITY IN THE AUTISM COMMUNITY

For years now, I've been a consultant specializing in counseling teams challenged in understanding those with different ways of being, including autism. I've been privy to interact with autistic individuals of great spiritual brilliance with a beauty that emanates from within and radiates outwardly—a mutual "knowingness," if you will. Some of these persons or their families graciously affirmed my initial perceptions of a spiritual connection. Their anecdotes underscored the heightened awareness, innate gentleness, and exquisite sensitivity in a number of those with autism; that is, a capacity to perceive all things seen and unseen. For some, these blessings came in the form of "Gifts of the Spirit," of which I had experienced as a child, read about, or was open to. Examples reportedly range from knowing what someone is thinking before it is said; foretelling future events that come to fruition; and enjoying special, unspoken bonds with animals. Still others are said to have perceived visions of grandparents and other loved ones in Spirit, or even communed with angels—abilities seemingly reserved for Old World saints and prophets.

But on reconsideration, this "higher-vibration" capacity of the senses is indeed consistent with the acute, often overwhelming autistic sensitivities to sight, smell, taste, touch, and hearing. There are, in fact, some individuals with autism that even react to positive ion changes in weather systems—a condition called serotonin stress reaction—which can wreak havoc on their nervous systems. In 2002, the American Academy of Neurology reported on research by scientists from the Medical College of Georgia, the University of South Carolina, and the Downtown VA Medical Center in Augusta, Georgia, that centered upon computerized brain imaging in persons with autism. Their findings of smaller but multiply-more-than-average minicolumns, a basic organizational unit of brain cells, was equable with this chronic state of over-arousal thought to affect one's capacity to discriminate between competing sensory information.

Concurrent with my own spiritual rediscovery, and shortly before the 2002 publication of my first book about the autistic experience, I began to feel compelled or "pulled" to embark upon another book. The new project would cover this little-known facet of autism that, until now, has been largely "closeted," undiscussed, or dismissed altogether. This book is the result: a purely informational offering not intended to promulgate any new program, method, or intervention. It does, though, invite the reader to consider alternative possibilities in viewing autism through an entirely different lens.

The clinical definition of autism is not family—or individual—friendly. It is, unfortunately, oftentimes an indicator of one's perceived deficits rather than one's strengths, gifts, and abilities. Many parents tell me their child's diagnosis is a "death sentence." Some are deeply embittered or resentful of their child's autism and the confusing, sometimes violent, behaviors that may ensue. This is a great disparity in the field. The focus so frequently becomes how to best manage and control those with autism for the sake of conformity and "normalcy" that we become oblivious to the obvious. And the obvious is the extraordinary and monumental offerings provided by those who are inherently gentle and exquisitely sensitive.

Above all, we must shatter the stereotype that those with autism *necessarily* experience intellectual impairment (i.e., mental retardation) as a direct result of the autism. If you subscribe to this concept, I will respectfully request that you suspend your disbelief because my mantra is "always presume intellect." I would also encourage your further comprehension of autism by directing you to my book, *Demystifying the Autistic Experience*. (This volume also contains additional autobiographical information for those interested in my story.)

From a theological perspective, if our souls are on a path of perpetual learning in a journey toward attaining spiritual perfection, it may be congruent that those individuals with the greatest life challenges are among the most advanced of souls. Angela, a very young girl with autistic attributes, observed, "I pray Heaven has a plan for my life. God loves people with lives like mine." Spiritually-elevated souls like Angela's have selectively chosen to be so challenged in collaboration with a Higher Power. (No wonder people with autism often use the analogy of feeling like strangers on a foreign planet—the distance from their spiritual tier to our earthly plane is vast.) While not autistic, witness the triumphs of Helen Keller, young *Heartsongs* author Matthew Stepanek, and others over extraordinary adversity. Where so many other facets of human endurance are concerned, their souls have already "been there, done that." Dr. Michael Newton supports this contention in his book, *Journey of Souls*, when he writes, "Souls in a high state of advancement are often found in humble circumstances on Earth."

I speculate that many such individuals are closely protected by divine intervention during their earthly mentoring and tutorship. Please don't mistake me. I'm not suggesting that *every* person with autism possesses multisensory abilities; I don't know this to be true. But, in my experience, there *is* a magnificent preponderance of persons who do share this common thread. In reflection of Dr. Newton's research, I also suggest this may be true of many individuals who are significantly challenged in other respects. In fact, by reading this book, you may well be able to extract the word "autism" and insert any number of developmental differences and have the message remain the same; it's just that my focus here is autism.

Does this mean that all people with autism are "angelic" in their perfection and can do no wrong? Of course not. Many communicate in ways we don't understand such that we misinterpret and mislabel such outpourings as severe "behaviors." The point is that we are *all* frail and faulty human beings charged with making the best of our lives, learning to connect with and touch others along the way. And the capacity for such inner-connectedness is hard-wired into every one of us. In his article "Fools of God," self-advocate Nick Pentzell is adamant when making this distinction, disallowing do-gooders' glorification, vilification, or pretentious pity:

> The way people react in my presence often reveals something of their religious attitudes about disability. On the negative end, I have been seen as a punishment from God, a conduit for something demonic or supernatural by people who haven't understood my method of communication, a burden to test the faith of my caregivers, and a soul who incurred bad karma in past lives and now suffers autism. The positive views are just as preposterous; I am an emanation of Christ, an angel, a miracle, a holy innocent, and a Fool of God.

Pentzell's reality-check perspective serves to balance our overzealousness and contain our impulse to fawn artificially.

My critics will invalidate my credentials and accuse me of attempting to prey upon the fragile emotions of families desperate for a positive rationale to explain their child's autism. However, there is *absolutely nothing* I'm exploring here that's not already well known to individuals with autism, their families, friends, and relatives—albeit usually in the context of clandestine conversation. In my travels, I have invited audience members to remain after each of my autism presentations to participate in a discussion about autism and spirituality, and, inevitably, about a dozen or so people stay behind. I am never disappointed when, given a safe and comfortable forum in which to speak openly, parents and caregivers absolve themselves of amazing, joyful anecdotes, believing all the while to have experienced them in isolation. One such anecdote was shared by Carol from central Indiana:

> When the World Trade Center towers came down on September 11, 2001, I went to bed horrified, fearful, and angry. Then I remembered that Steven had not said his prayers. My son was only nine years old at the time and has high-functioning autism. Steven's prayer rocked me to the core. He said all of his "usuals" about blessings and family, then he asked God to forgive Osama bin Laden for killing people! I was speechless. This little boy who has struggled so much saw the heart of God and how saddened God was at the destruction of so many lives. I came away renewed in my own faith, especially in the amazing mind of my little boy.

This kind of affirming corroboration occurs no matter my geographic locale.

I must tell you that there are those persons with such great gifts who have cautioned me against pursuing this topic. One beloved friend with autism even advised that it was better for him and others to remain silent about it. He doesn't want to risk antagonizing others' perceptions by fueling stereotypes of "autistic behavior," only to be explained away as delusions or psychotic episodes and medicated accordingly. To those who so wish to blame that which they cannot readily explain on mental illness, please know that being autistic *does not* automatically make one mentally ill. Mental illness must be diagnosed by clusters of symptoms unusual to that person—not by isolated or sporadic incidents. Autism, itself, is not a mental illness, but mental illness in those already vulnerable, predisposed to being exquisitely sensitive, and inherently gentle is a very real possibility *separate* from autism. Before jumping to hasty and harmful conclusions, please become educated about the most prevalent symptoms of mental health issues in people with autism: depression, bipolar disorder, anxiety, and post-traumatic stress disorder. (I've excluded obsessive-compulsive disorder because I feel it is misunderstood and over-prescribed; some individuals' repetitive actions or verbalizations are often a deliberate focal point in reaction to painful irritants and other environmental stimuli naturally filtered by neurotypical folks.)

Others with autism have arbitrarily acknowledged the existence of their spiritual gifts but are, understandably, blasé or not terribly interested in giving the subject much airtime. It's there, but not overly significant in lieu of paramount issues such as self-advocacy, civil rights, and the tireless endeavor of general acceptance.

My purpose for pursuing this topic is to enlighten others about a unique and glorious facet of the autistic experience. It is in keeping with our collective pursuit of shattering myths and stereotypes about such experiences being a product of intellectual impairment or mental illness. And it speaks to the principle that people with different ways of being are often *our* teachers, here to guide our understanding of compassion, sensitivity, and unconditional love—the most vital lessons of the human condition. Many are possessed of a divine spiritual connection of which we must be open to learning about. It is time. Andrew Bloomfield, a Canadian poet with autism, summarizes, "In my mind, loving people is loving God. I want to be able to teach others but not be a guinea pig. I like to think I can inspire others."

I have strived to present very sensitive information in an accurate and truthful manner. I have taken great care to portray personal stories in a gentle way while concurrently offering validation. Many of the individuals involved have chosen to use pseudonyms or just first names as a protective measure. However, we have no reason to believe that their stories are not authentic. Self-advocates, parents, and caregivers of people with autism can have intensely complex lives. I don't believe for a moment that any of the good people whom I met and interviewed, or who contacted me by phone or email, gave of their precious time for personal gain or deliberately misled me. They've been most courageous to risk sharing private testimony to benefit us all. Our goal will have been achieved if their stories ring true as affirmations for parents, caregivers, and others who realize the blessed qualities of their loved ones.

I also bring to the subject my background in supporting people with different ways of being since 1987. Simultaneous with compiling this volume I immersed myself in research, including the invaluable illuminations of the most reputable and revered spiritual leaders and visionaries. Their writings have either validated my own work or provided me with concepts of which to aspire. All bear the same universal message: live to love.

I realize that spiritual giftedness in people with autism is a delicate and controversial subject. When we view this possibility from a global perspective, we establish a starting point for growth and change to occur—if we can be open to it. Often, our fear of the unknown precludes us from accepting that which we cannot readily discern. However, we don't question our capacity to give and receive love, yet we love without factual evidence of love's authenticity. We can prove the brain's existence but not that of the human mind. Our holiest of religious beliefs may be regarded in the same light; disbelievers seek tangible proof. Similarly, the multisensory blessings of the person with autism should not be so casually explained away simply because traditional science finds them immeasurable. For such blessings are measured only in the heart.

A Path to
Opportunity

one

Making Miracles

⌘

When a family receives a diagnosis of autism for their son or daughter, for some there occurs a death. The death is the loss of the person the child was envisioned to be. Some doctors are not helpful, gentle, or sensitive in presenting the diagnosis, causing the feeling of loss to be reinforced for families. The diagnosis may offer relieving confirmation of suspicions about a child's growth, development, and interactions with others. But the diagnosis may also come with confusing clinical jargon; deficit-based information about the child's supposed limitations of intellectual capacity and abilities—and a hopeless prognosis for the future.

A grieving process may begin in which the dream for whom the child was supposed to be gives way to worries and concerns over his or her way of being in life and the responsibility for perpetual caregiving. Mourn not, for the dream needn't be surrendered in its entirety. It needs only to be modified to better match the unique personality traits and abilities of the person with autism. In redefining the dream, that individual will surely bear unexpected, surprising nuances that will be fulfilling and rewarding. Because of this, many parents and caregivers realize their lives have been forever altered in profound, loving ways. They are different, yes, better people for parenting the individual with autism.

There are those who believe that many individuals with differences are predominantly chaste in their way of being. Some with autism have not fully integrated with their bodies and it is speculated that a compensation exists, creating a special alignment with their subconscious mind or spiritual selves. This aptitude for accessing a non-ending stream of consciousness may cause division with the physical body, a neurological motor-and-spatial disconnect. A paradox results that emphasizes aesthetics and high thought over physicality— the reverse from our "norm" of conformity. Because of this shift in orientation, those with autism may hold capacity for spiritual connectedness, heightened awareness, and exquisite sensitivity beyond what is considered typical. These abilities are gifts and blessings. Cathy Boyle of Winchester, Massachusetts, mom to son Terry, developed what is thought to be the first Catholic religious education course for kids with autism based upon her belief that they could "intuitively understand the concept of God and draw comfort from belonging to a spiritual community." Certainly, in the Creator's plan nothing happens by chance. Experiences of relaying unspoken thoughts, forecasting certain circumstances, or even communing with Spirit are all, then, merely extensions of that spiritual connectedness—not coincidences or overactive imagination. This is natural, not supernatural.

For validation, one need only look to the published works of young Marshall Ball, a silent child who expresses himself through typing his astoundingly gorgeous thoughts and poetry about God, life, and those dearest to him. Marshall writes in a sage manner of comprehension that is light-years beyond his chronological age. More than one grateful admirer of Marshall's has observed that he is surely an "old soul" gifted to educate the world. Thirty-seven-year-old Canadian poet Andrew Bloomfield made his interest and understanding of God's presence known to his family despite bearing the label of "severe autism." Taken unaware, Andrew's mother remarked, "What's interesting to us is that we never talked about all this as he was growing up, and he never had any Sunday school or church experience. It was Andrew himself who started using the terms 'spirituality' and 'soul.'"

In preparation for this book, a mom named Teri sent insightful information about her son that supports this concept:

> My son Jarrod is autistic and is ten years old. He has had very little formal religious training, but his concept of God is better than most people I know. He will spontaneously request that we pray and has given my husband a lecture (in his own way) about praying and going to church and reading the Bible. He just "gets" the whole God concept and incorporates it into his life with no historical or current prompting.

Reneé, another mom, echoed these sentiments when she wrote of her six-year-old son, Gabriel.

> Many times, at three years old, he would touch people on their head and "bless" them. I have a picture of him in front of the statue of Mary at two years old.

> He is looking at the statue as if it were real…Sometimes he puts on my nightgown and says things like, "Mary, go to Jerusalem." He is pretending to be a pastor. How odd that a child with severe autism could pretend such things. But what is the real picture here? In my opinion, he is called to spirituality and is gifted in some area. He is always calm at church and watches and listens intently to the pastor.

Mary affirmed her own son's call to spirituality when she shared her amazing story. Never deeply religious, she and her husband became angry at God for being "punished" with a child less than perfect. The family now realizes that sixteen-year-old Andrew is a gift from God, and because of him they have found their faith on a level not previously attainable.

> In fall 1997, Andrew began watching what we called "the Catholic channel." After school, he would turn on the rosary; in the morning, he would listen to a Franciscan monk speak about the apostles; and whenever possible, he would watch Mass, both English and Latin. We didn't think much of this until later. Andrew rarely speaks in more than three-word sentences, and then it's usually to ask for juice or a snack. In late fall, he began asking us to pray at dinner, and one evening when we were out at his favorite restaurant, he asked us to join hands while he said the entire Lord's Prayer. We had never said the Lord's Prayer with him! On other occasions he would come up to me and say, "Mommy, may the

grace of our Lord Jesus Christ be with you always."

One morning while I was upstairs getting ready for work, listening to the news on TV, Andrew came up and changed the channel to a monk who was talking about St. Andrew. This monk spoke of how St. Andrew was the "quiet" saint who was the first to meet Jesus and brought others to him—how St. Andrew always worked quietly in the background bringing others to the faith. What struck me while listening to this was that I remembered that when I was pregnant with Andrew, I knew immediately that there was no other name for our baby than Andrew; I had trouble even considering a girl's name.

The media, cynics, and scientists may oppose or refute the connection between spiritual giftedness and individuals with autism who are, in the parlance of some, "afflicted sufferers stricken by a devastating disorder." Certain prejudices and authoritarian contentions stem from comparisons in quality of life, using what is considered "normal" and neuro-typical as the measuring stick of fulfillment. Those who would seek to clinically examine, analyze, dissect, and disqualify the recipients of spiritual gifts pose obstacles for the autism community's faith and belief system. Besides, how can that which is unanticipated and spontaneous ever be measured? As a poet, grandmother, and person with an autistic experience, Devlyn Lighthawk shared her thoughts about this struggle.

Yes it is a spiritual gift, but those not in understanding of the truth of "spiritual" can hardly see the truth of "us." Knowing that telepathy is just us talking, beyond words, you know. Harder to get that understanding into the minds of "science," "technology," "industrialized," "educated" interactors of mundane. [They] cannot see or believe that between the sand and sea lie universes and times unknown and unseen.

In his landmark book, *The Seat of the Soul,* author Gary Zukav devotes a chapter to the subject of reverence, which he defines as a way of being, a perception of the soul, and "a natural aspect of authentic empowerment because the soul reveres all of Life." Zukav's further discussion of reverence is especially like my personal perception of people with autism, and how they might interpret the world. Zukav writes:

An attitude of reverence is the atmosphere, the environment, in which the multisensory personality evolves. It is a sense of richness and fullness and intimacy of being. It creates compassion and acts of kindness. Without reverence, without the perception of holiness of all things, the world becomes cold and barren, mechanical and random at the same time, and this creates experiences of alienation and acts of violence. It is not natural for us to live without reverence, because that separates us from the basic energy of the soul.

Most importantly, Zukav continues, "An attitude of reverence facilitates the transition from the logic and understanding of the five-sensory human to the higher order of logic and understanding of the multisensory human, because…this higher order of logic and understanding originates in the heart." As you will read, this has had personal resonance. Once I confronted myself and all my inherent faults and frailties, I began to grow toward a higher order of logic and understanding. In turn, this began to manifest outwardly with glowing results. Most of my dear friends who are exquisitely sensitive beings have already attained this higher order. They demonstrate reverence naturally despite ongoing hardships and obstacles.

The challenge is to first recognize and embrace this concept. Many parents, caregivers, and educators already do. They are deeply appreciative of the compassion and understanding their loved ones offer simply by being in the world. They already recognize that many people with differences are *our* teachers. For example, young Geoff of Rochester, New York, like so many others, matter-of-factly informed his parents that he *chose* them before birth, designating the family dynamics with planful intent. Empowered by a strong sense of understanding, such caregivers are well on their way to reciprocating reverence. Does this mean that caregivers who don't accord this understanding are incorrect in their thinking? Note that this section of the book is titled "*A* Path to Opportunity," not "*The* Path…" But some caregivers are so driven to "fix," "cure," "remediate," and "make normal" their loved ones that they overlook the purest of truths.

In their article "Autism: Declaring War," Frewsburg, New York, parents Dan and Toni Gage write of their consuming obsession to eradicate their son Danny's autism, spawned by a mixture of guilt, inadequacy, and an all-out assault to conquer the "enemy." Theirs was the mindset that "Failure will not be an option. We must 'cure' our son!" (In contrast, another little boy, six-year-old Dilon Stutesman, is nearly apologetic when explaining, "You can't shut the autism off, I've tried.") The Gages finally reached a spiritual juncture at which point they disarmed, realizing that waging battle was futile. "Autism is not our enemy. Our beautiful son was born with something labeled autism. He was also born with blue eyes and light brown hair. We would no sooner change his eye color. They are part of his composition just like autism is. We were searching so diligently for a way to 'cure' him or make him 'normal.' The truth is, we love him just the way he is." At last the Gages understood: "Victory is already ours and had been all along…and so we have put our armor away because we realized that we don't want or need to wage a war on autism anymore. Instead, we would rather live a peaceful coexistence which, after all, is exactly what we are wishing for Danny and his peers."

For every individual who is embraced by his caregivers as a work of art—a person naturally possessed of great and radiant beauty—there exist many others who are waiting patiently in silence for their caregivers to reach a similar understanding. This does not negate the importance of supporting the autistic one toward achieving functional communication, learning how to care for oneself, comprehending societal expectations, higher education, and holistic wellness. This is a spiritual position and a sound prospect by which to abide no matter the supposed intellectual difference attributed to another.

In considering those specifically with autism, it has been

estimated that 70 to 80 percent have a concurrent diagnosis (among others) of intellectual impairment. That is, mental retardation. My response, and that of leagues of other supporters and advocates, is to state, quite candidly, "That is an untruth." It's a myth and stereotype perpetuated by those limited to diagnostic tools and the parameters of their own thinking and experience. Others appreciate the concept of intelligence versus *wisdom*, but there are advantages in accessing "the system" if a diagnosis of intellectual impairment is ascribed. However, any one of us would fail an Intelligence Quotient examination if we were without speech, and given no advance knowledge of what to expect. Think if you were completely unprepared; a total stranger administered the test in an unfamiliar or uncomfortable environment; and you were being asked to comply with odd, purposeless, or demeaning tasks never before requested of you. Such is the fate of many that have been diagnosed as autistic.

Where does this leave us in terms of our understanding of autism? At present, the unknown far outweighs the known. What we *do* know about autism is that it prevails worldwide. It has only become acceptable and less stigmatizing to make an autism diagnosis in little more than the past decade. Fifteen years ago one in every 10,000 children in America was estimated to be autistic. Since then, there has been a drastic, unaccountable jump. *Time* magazine, May 6, 2002, reported, "the latest studies…suggest that as many as one in 150 kids age ten and younger may be affected by autism or a related disorder." Today, the federal Centers for Disease Control and Prevention (CDC) estimates that one in every 166 children has autism, averaging nearly 425,000 children nationwide—this is in addition to the CDC's assertion that one in every six children has a neurodevelopmental disorder. According to the CDC website (www.cdc.gov), fifty-three infants born daily in the United States were diagnosed with autism in 2003, or roughly 19,000 infants per year. And 2004 CDC statistics indicate that autism has increased over ten-fold in only seven years consistent with the latest numbers released by the U.S. Department of Education. The school population went from 12,222 in 1992–1993 to 118,602 for 2003–2004. The state of Wisconsin showed the largest rate of increase at an astronomical 14,170 percent. And these numbers don't even begin to capture the adult population. The configuration of statistics appears endless.

The seeming "explosion" of children identified with autism (now more common than Down Syndrome or child-hood cancer) is balanced, in part, by the vast numbers of adults with autism of all ages who have a diagnosis only of "mental retardation." In the introduction, I indicate that one of the diagnostic criteria for autism is challenges in the area of communication. This means that many persons so diag-nosed are unable to produce speech or have limited vocal capabilities. Perhaps they make vocalizations that are not readily discernable. When someone doesn't speak, we may not receive him or her as our peer because of this "surface" limitation. In addition to autism, they may receive clinical diagnoses of mildly, severely, or profoundly retarded. Indeed, many families have told me they've been bluntly informed their loved ones don't have anything of value to say regardless.

ALWAYS PRESUME INTELLECT

My plea is that we shift our thinking of the autistic experience as one would consider a person with Cerebral Palsy. The
person's body or outward "shell" works in ways that are
unreliable and atypical. That person may be unable to speak
or gesticulate, or may require total assistance in all self-care
skills (eating, bathing, dressing). The person with Cerebral
Palsy may even be unable to ambulate without support of a
cane, a walker, or a wheelchair. It does *not* follow that the person's intellect is *necessarily* impaired to the same degree. Now,
parallel this concept with autism in which an individual's
physical limitations may appear identical. The mannerisms
projected by the person inhabiting an autistic shell may readily mimic what some label an inferior way of being. While the
neurology of one's *brain* may be compromised, resulting in
brain-body disconnects and motor-control misfires, this does
not refute the inner will of one's *mind* and *Spirit*. When we
say of the person with autism, "When I look into his eyes, I
can tell someone's in there," it's because *there is* someone in
there—a vibrant, intelligent human being! Why would anyone choose to adopt a different position?

Similarly, when the same individual gazes back, peering
deeply into the eyes of a caregiver, it is for the purpose of
discerning one's very soul. Lori, from Lancaster,
Pennsylvania, shared her capacity for determining those who
are sincere as well as those disingenuous. She said it takes her
one second to figure out if someone is kind upon first meeting
them. "I look for kindness in their eyes. I see into the heart."
Lori further described this unique process, distinguishing
personalities through colors evident to her: "Colors, certain

colors signify kindness. Blue is kindness. Black is unkindness. Red is being bad. I see red when people are bad…I think Heaven shows through self."

I have no empirical data to substantiate my position about a belief in intellectual competence in those with autism, only rich anecdotal testimony. However, far from exacting science, all of psychology and psychiatry—the root of most autism treatments—is also speculative. But, I *have* experienced being with others who felt safe and comfortable enough to actively demonstrate their true personalities and powerful wisdom, some through their actions or alternative methods of communication. As such, I have been blessed to sit in the presence of greatness.

Where does one begin? In the introduction, I state that my golden rule or mantra is "always presume intellect." *This is the proper response to autism.* Does it mean we now have the right to expect that autistic individuals yield some profound intellect not yet revealed? Will they be able to understand complex curriculums beyond what they've already been taught? Or should we raise our expectations of acceptable conduct and then blame that person if they are not fulfilled to fruition? No. Presuming intellect is about belief in competence. It is as simple as interacting and being with others in the same ways that you would welcome from anyone else. In short, do unto others as you would have them do unto you.

Presuming intellect implores us to understand that our traditional concept of "intelligence"—which may truly be dormant and unchallenged—must be tempered with an appreciation of individuals' good and great *wisdom.* It means talking the talk *and* walking the walk in true and genuine demonstration of respect. Chiefly, that includes not speaking about someone in front of them as if they were not present at all. (This also includes sharing praiseful remarks with others without first obtaining the individual's permission, akin to the embarrassment of being surprised with a round of "Happy Birthday" in the middle of a crowded restaurant.) You would be amazed at how easily people find it to talk about others in front of them—often in disparaging terms—so that it has become an unconscious habit. I am sometimes asked if I subscribe to behavior management. Yes, I believe in behavior management; I believe in managing the behavior of those around the individual with autism in an effort to teach these most salient concepts from the "inside out."

Presuming intellect also requires that we speak to someone with the belief that they understand what is being said. It means using fewer words, and allowing the individual time to process what we've just said. It means abandoning our own agenda and showing regard for an individual's personal, physical space by not intruding upon it suddenly and without warning, as so many caregivers have been trained to do (e.g., grabbing someone's face to command eye contact with the words "Look at me!" Remember, that if the scenario were reversed, we'd call it physical aggression). It also means acquiescing our demands and rigid expectations so that fair compromise permits temporary release, and people are allowed the freedom to be their autistic selves, as they are. And it means direct confrontation with the three most powerful words any of us can say about ourselves: "I was wrong."

Rae and her family learned this valuable lesson the hard way. She reflected, "You know, my daughter always told me not to talk about Michael [Rae's son] in front of him when he was very young. We thought he didn't understand. We were wrong. It's so easy to slip into that mode. I've seen staff do it too. Folks think that they don't listen or understand, but they most certainly do." All the wiser, Rae has since tirelessly founded an organization, Autism Living and Working, which actively engages Pennsylvania state government to "help people with autism form and sustain households, hold jobs, and contribute to community life, through individual support and accommodations."

An audience member once asked for whom do I *not* presume intellect. My response was, "No one." I will not surrender this belief. Once I'm so arrogant to believe I have the authority to judge another, others will qualify it. They'll suggest, "Well what about her…or him?" and the purpose of my work becomes null and void. (Lest we forget, in our not-too-distant history, *all* persons with Cerebral Palsy were deemed "retarded," and even left-handed people were thought deviant.)

If, in reading this, you know in your heart you are guilty of committing the above transgressions—no matter how subtle—in having been disrespectful, unpresuming of intellect, or not as gentle or sensitive as you could be, congratulations. There is no shame in confessing this unto yourself. Only liberation awaits, for this is the first miracle.

THE FIRST MIRACLE

The first miracle is self-reflection. When you make this acknowledgment, you take your first step toward a path of opportunity. A similar catalyst causes anyone to self-initiate in order to right wrongs. We've witnessed this anytime someone apologizes to us genuinely. In more complex situations, an abusive spouse or parent adopts anger management or a substance user seeks clinical and spiritual treatment. Such actions require introspective thought, "soul searching" as some might say.

But self-reflection alone is not enough. Please complete the miracle by taking the next step in making things right. The next step is to privately, gently, and respectfully approach the individual you know you've hurt or offended—intentionally or not. Offer your humble, genuine, sincere, and heartfelt apologies. If you do this truly, the next miracle will occur.

THE SECOND MIRACLE

The second miracle is forgiveness. And you *will be* forgiven. I can state this with conviction because I have received countless in-person testimonies, phone calls, letters, and emails from those who assumed responsibility of self-reflection and made things right by confessing their wrongs. When this happens, truly miraculous occurrences can transpire. Will this cause someone to shed her autistic attributes through some divine act? Of course not, and if that is your sole motivation you have misinterpreted the purpose and intent of this work.

People tell me frequently that they perceived their relationship with those in their care to be on one level or in a good place. But they discover, upon seeking absolution, that the relationship soars and attains a plateau they never before dreamed possible. This is the miracle of forgiveness.

Valentine's Day 2001 was my first consultation with Clint and his mom, Janet, during which we discussed such measures. Upon appealing to Clint with gentle reverence,

Janet was witness to immediate changes in their relationship and camaraderie. He was still the same person who did not speak and engaged in repetitive movements. But they now interacted differently, and she perceived something awaken in his eyes. Nearly two years later, Clint's case manager, Teri, contacted me to further validate the tremendous power of that simple act.

> I need to tell you, the changes for Clint and for his family have been miraculous. I recently completed a timeline for Clint [a linear, chronological overview of his life] and it was wonderful to see the changes continuing that began when you spoke to Mrs. B. [Clint's mom] about talking to Clint when she assists him, apologizing to him for not always understanding his abilities, and giving him proper credit for what he knows.
>
> While we were working on the timeline, the obvious communication and respect that is now very much evident in their relationship was amazing to see. Clint was very much involved in directing how the days went because now the people around him, following his mother's example, are asking him what he wants and standing back, waiting for him to communicate his wants in his life.
>
> As we reviewed and talked about all of the ways Clint has been a wonderful communicator of his needs (we just weren't adept at listening), and how he has always found ways to cope with what was happening around him when he wasn't in control of it, he came over and stood in front of me and gazed

into my eyes for a long moment, conveying silently a combination of "Thank you for finally realizing that," and "It's about time you all figured that out!"

It was a great couple of days and really wonderful to see the good things that happened between the two of them once Mrs. B. saw the wonderful gifts her son has. I just wanted to share that with you since it all stems from the understanding you helped her to find when you talked with them.

A similar renewal occurred for Debbie when she approached her teenage son Scott to make amends and offer apology. He listened carefully, and patiently waited until she had finished her little speech. Then he lovingly, succinctly observed, "You're so sweet." Debbie told me with tearful joy that it was rare for Scott to speak, if at all.

Both Clint and Scott presented me with their original works of art as gifts of appreciation, for which I was humbled. Debbie wrote:

I was preparing Scott for the fact that there would be a few nights that I would not be home to meet him as he got off the bus. I told him it was because I was going to see the man who helped me understand so much about autism. I told him I would like to give you a gift that would tell you how much you have helped us. Scott got up and brought me [a hand-painted and decorated mask of his face]. He handed it to me and said, "How about *this*?" I must say he again blew me away. After I was done crying, I told him how very appropriate it was. His response was, "I know it."

Bill, you have helped me to begin unmasking autism. For this I will always be profoundly grateful. You have given me an insight into my son's world and you gave me the key I needed to occasionally join him there. I have found it to be a truly beautiful place. Again, thank you for all of your help and your patience in explaining it so I, too, can be a messenger to all who are ready to hear.

I recently presented in a very rural location in which behavior management was the exclusively-accepted practice to support autism. This made the task of communicating my beliefs very difficult. In particular, there were two behavior specialists present who frequently challenged me, intensely skeptical of my motives and my own authenticity. Regrettably, they were so steeped in their ways that they blocked reflecting upon other possibilities or hearing the true message. They left midway through the day. Although my program received favorable response, I doubted myself, feeling I had failed them. However a compensation did occur: within little more than twenty-four hours, I received a message from Linda, also in attendance that day. At the request of a friend who passed away, Linda was now surrogate mom to two boys with autism, ages eleven and fourteen. She offered a powerful validation when she emailed to tell me the outcome of having enacted the first two miracles:

Your talk made me rethink many of my ways of talking to the boys. I immediately told them about you and

that you had made me see things differently. I talked
to them separately and told them that I was so sorry
if I had made them feel badly or uncomfortable and
that I would try to be better. My older boy, Bill, who
does not talk much said, "That's okay, Linda. I love you
very much." I am crying again now. That is a great gift
you have given me. I appreciate it very much.

Another mom told me she experienced something similar
when she concluded her confession. Although her son does
not speak, he sat and began to applaud her soundly as if to
communicate, "This is the moment for which I've been waiting—Mom finally gets it!"

In yet another instance, I counseled a team supporting a
fourteen-year-old young man about presuming his intellect
and interacting with a belief in his competence. Immediately
following the discussion, the young man spontaneously rose
up and, without any prompting, walked to our refreshment
table, and methodically, carefully served each person seated at
the table a cookie on a napkin—something he'd never done
before.

The pledge of renewed respect must be demonstrated
every moment of every day, especially in the presence of the
person who offers us sweet redemption—and beyond. It is a
process that requires time and discipline to achieve. Losing
our temper, crying in frustration, or saying things we wish we
hadn't are all part of the human experience. The difference
comes in how we now approach our loved ones to express it.
Armed with the knowledge of this new perspective, we are
better able to tame and refine our own reactions.

Each one of us is a messenger who can alter and transform the perceptions of others. The pledge of renewed respect must also include advocating for those not yet able to advocate for themselves in the presence of others. It means *gently and respectfully* requesting that others discontinue the practice of being disrespectful, unpresuming of intellect, or not as gentle or sensitive as they could be. It means being firm, thoughtful, and creative when intercepting family, relatives and neighbors, educators and therapists, and doctors who demonstrate disrespect in the presence of a loved one. It is a learning time for them too.

THE THIRD MIRACLE

The third miracle is perpetuate the message. As you've read, Scott's mom, Debbie, understood the responsibility of the third miracle *as a direct result of witnessing the first two miracles occur* when she wrote, "I, too, can be a messenger to all who are ready to hear." In a powerful display of her heart's clarity, it came to her as a natural and logical progression without anyone else recommending it. Debbie is now fully aware in her role as an agent of change and an ambassador of goodwill.

What exactly is "the ripple effect" where people with autism are concerned? It is, quite simply, what occurs when we effectively invoke the three miracles of self-reflection, forgiveness, and perpetuity of the message. The aftereffect of our demonstration of love and vows of renewed respect flows outwardly like concentric ripples of the surface of a pond. The further the ripples grow in size and distance, the more they intersect and connect with like ripples. It is the same when we advocate on behalf of loved ones, advocate for ourselves, or join with others to share our heartfelt spirit. If we put good things "out there," it follows that good things will eventually overlap with our thinking and our way of being, thereby providing us with validations, affirmations, and spiritual nourishment to press onward. This is not some New Age mumbo jumbo, nor is it rocket science; it truly is a commitment that can unfold with amazing outcomes. You *can* create a transformation. I'm living proof of it, as you'll see.

Perpetuating the message will not be easy. If it were, we wouldn't have the opportunity to learn the depth of our love and the strength of our conviction. Both will be vigorously tried and tested. You may be met with violent resistance from those who refuse to presume intellect. Bear in mind that many people who use derogatory "us and them" language aren't even hearing themselves, or feel it's within their purview to speak with an authority that further distances our humanity from those with autism. Imagine being the autistic one, charged with defending your own self-worth in the face of such adversity *every day*.

But this is not about our personal likes, preferences, and choices. Be neither intimidated nor tenuous. We have made a vow of commitment to a Higher Authority. Remember this: *creating authentic change means risking doing the right thing.* Think of the hideous inequality that would exist if no one ever risked doing the right thing: women would be unable to vote, people of color would be without civil rights, and persons of a same-sex orientation would not have achieved some of the advances made in recent history. I am optimistic that we are *all* on a learning curve, evolving toward an understanding that human differences are inconsequential where love reigns. Let's recognize that we are all just human souls.

For those times that cause us doubt and skepticism, we need only consider for whom we are advocating—in this instance, the person with autism. It is a gift to draw strength from the gentle sweetness of each individual's will, just as you would rely upon the strength of any beloved supporter. It is there for us to use if we request it sincerely. Do not hesitate to do this by approaching your loved one and asking. Request to silently draw upon their spiritual will in arduous moments, even if they aren't present just then. The times that are challenging and even frustrating will enable us to better appreciate those times when the third miracle occurs. Recognize when you have gently enlightened someone who is now in a position to perpetuate the message to others.

A Spiritual Response

Recently, when asked to comment on the soaring incidence of autism, Dr. Harvey Fineberg, president of the Institute of Medicine, of the National Academy of Sciences, conceded, "There's definitely a high number of cases diagnosed with autism...No one knows with certainty what part of the increase is genuine, a genuine increase in numbers, and what part is from increased recognition of people who were already there but not previously recognized." Journalists such as Dan Olmstead, UPI's Consumer Health editor, point to the inexplicable: "...the idea that autism is primarily a genetic disorder doesn't hold up. No genetic illness could rise so rapidly. But if there have always been people with autism in reasonably similar numbers, then the idea that some new trigger—vaccines, for example—is behind autism begins to look implausible if not impossible." Even the work of Leo Kanner, the "father of modern child psychiatry" and the world's foremost autism researcher, yields discrepancies when one considers that, within the first fifteen years after defining the autism diagnosis, Kanner identified only 150 cases—this from children referred to his office at Johns Hopkins University from North America, South America, and South Africa. UPI's Dan Olmstead summarizes, "No matter how you slice or dice the diagnostic categories, something doesn't compute—how can there be half a million children with Autism Spectrum Disorders living in the United States today, when the man who identified the disorder could only find 150 in the first fifteen years?" In response to Olmstead's query, there remains an explanation that is as relevant as any other.

In this author's opinion, the seemingly sudden and mysterious surge of children identified with autism is a reflection of our recent history. As the world requires more love, compassion, and tolerance amidst ever-mounting global concerns, the numbers of such children silently and surely grow exponentially. This is our Creator's purposeful plan to refocus us on the importance of reverence for all of humanity. After all, so many individuals with autism are, at the core of their very being, all about love. They can be infinitely patient in demonstrating that love. In fact, the two phrases most frequently communicated to me upon first connecting with others with autism are, "I love you," and "I'm not retarded."

Making miracles on a path to opportunity requires self-introspection, a thorough examination of the heart's motives for being. Ensure that your way of being with someone with autism is predicated upon a safe, trusting, and loving relationship. Provide natural and comfortable structures and environments for learning, reciprocation, and growth. You can compel the person with autism to conform and comply by rigid management and control. But compliance for the sake of compliance does not equal success. Nor does it create a path to real and reciprocal growth. Which is the path of least resistance? Where is a true path to opportunity? A true path awaits you in this very moment.

two

Surrendering to Serendipity

∽

Before proceeding further, I wish to pause to allow you, the reader, to process what has gone before in order to gauge your comfort level. The premise I've shared to this point may have incited a mix of emotions that could range from outrage and indignation to solace and relief. If you are feeling resistant at this time, by all means discontinue reading now; things only get more intricate from here, and I certainly do not wish to impose upon anyone. My hope, of course, is that I've been preaching to the choir, but significant paradigm shifts can take time for some to mull and absorb fully. Where spirituality is concerned, many people come to embrace their creeds and personal beliefs over time.

When I was a little boy of about four years old, I remember sitting in a dentist office waiting room with my father, leafing through children's magazines until called for the appointment. On one page, a small elfin creature caught my attention and I begged my father to read me the story. It was about Jack Frost and how he went about the business of transforming all manner of flora with his snow crystals. Throughout the rest of our time in the office, I grilled my father for more information about this mystical entity. Despite his insistence that Jack Frost didn't actually exist, and in lieu of my father attempting to explain that the folklore was a metaphor, I remained nonplussed. As if by design, on the drive home from the dentist the temperature dropped significantly such that frost actually formed on the trees, leaves, and shrubs we passed. In the midst of this demonstration of nature's magic, my father was able to satisfy his original contentions. Of course I was terribly disappointed, having hoped to catch a glimpse of the elusive Jack Frost at work. I was crushed because I was disbelieving of the rational explanation for what had transpired.

Entertaining the notion of a Higher Power was similar for me. As a child, in my autistic mind, God was represented by the king on a playing card. Still, at a tender age I somehow grasped that God is pervasive and life eternal. At eight, I composed an insightful poem transcribed in meticulous penmanship:

God is everywhere.
Most people say Heaven is beautiful! But you live on and on.
Everywhere you look you see little buds sprouting.
God is making the buds sprout.
God is everywhere.

As an adolescent, concrete and literal-minded, I came to associate God with my discomfort of being in a crowded church or Sunday school filled with people with whom I neither felt nor wanted a connection. While I had a core belief grounded in God, I didn't practice that belief and—like any number of teenagers—questioned, dismissed, or tested it. I resented those who sought to blatantly impose their creed upon me, and I could not reconcile the incongruence of others whose transparent motivation for attending service was absolution of their bad acts the remaining days of the week. Why not just behave with decency every day, I wondered. Further, I was unable to separate the formality of a church environment with the individuality of a one-to-one relationship with God (as much an unseen entity as Jack Frost). It wasn't until I was older, more mature, that I understood what it meant to grow into a personal relationship with God. It was a *process*, and a slow epiphany.

For those who are as indifferent and dismissive of a spiritual center as I once was, consider that, more and more, traditional science and spirituality are becoming fused. In his 2004 bestselling book, *The Case for a Creator: A Journalist Investigates Scientific Evidence that Points Toward God*, Lee Strobel interviews at length Stephen C. Meyer, PhD, preeminent scientist, professor, and director of the Center for Science and Culture at the Discovery Institute in Seattle. Meyer contends that "…the major developments in science in the past five decades have been running in a strongly theistic direction.…Science *done right*, points toward God." Meyer goes on to poke holes in Darwinism and asserts that the universe would be totally incapable of supporting life if its expansion were altered by one part in either direction, indicating intelligent design.

SCIENCE, SPIRITUALITY, AND AUTISM

The gap between science and spirituality *and* autism may also be narrowing. Science is only just beginning to study the

DNA of individuals with autism in seeking genetic etiology. In December 2004, the National Institutes of Health spearheaded an international coalition comprised of government health agencies and private advocacy organizations that committed more than $21 million for research to identify the genes associated with autism spectrum disorders. How curious it is that, at the same time scientific research was strengthening the contention for the naturally-occurring biological causes of autism, a new book, *The God Gene* (and a concurrent *Time* cover story), speculated that human beings are genetically programmed for faith ("Does our DNA compel us to seek a higher power?"). Do individuals with autism have a greater likelihood to be genetically predisposed to both autism *and* spirituality? Consider the following intriguing parallels:

- Dr. Robert Cloninger, of St. Louis's Washington University Medical School, invented the self-transcendence scale, in part, to measure spirituality. It is based upon three components: self-forgetfulness, transpersonal identification, and mysticism. Interestingly, all three measurements crosswalk to traits of many individuals with autism. *Self-forgetfulness* involves becoming so utterly absorbed in work, a passion, a relationship, that one forgets time and place and sense of oneself on a regular basis—completely lacking in self-consciousness. Many of us experience this when immersed in creative ventures. But when considering consistencies of autism, does this concept sound familiar? In fact, the facet of self-transcendence that is self-forgetfulness is the very definition of autism, from the Greek word autos or "self." *Transpersonal identification* is a sense of connectedness to all things animate and inanimate in the entire universe employing all senses and emotions. This includes strong attachments to people, animals, and all of nature. Know someone with autism like this? Examples may be found throughout this volume. Finally, *mysticism* is defined as a fascination and openness to things that can't be explained by science— the very premise of this book where persons with autism are concerned.

• Neuroscientist Dr. Andrew Newberg, of the University of Pennsylvania School of Medicine, has used brain-imaging techniques to study the brains of his subjects as they meditate or pray. Blood flow measurement indicated the regions of the brain generating the feelings of his patients during their meditation. The rarest state of being, "Absolute Unitary Being," can be achieved, in part, in conjunction with rhythm such as a repetitive movement—not unlike the constant rocking, hand-flapping, or twirling of some individuals with autism! Solace is found in the controlled *sameness* of the repetition. (Neuro-typical persons naturally do this to some degree too; it just looks less exaggerated and more socially acceptable, like incessant leg shaking or hair twirling.) So many accuse those with autism of engaging in such "mindless, purposeless" activities, which I have always defended as functional, self-discovered coping mechanisms—a focal point to ward against the sensory-assaultive "real world." But now I'm thinking there's a dual purpose beyond even that in the way that those who mediate will focus on a word, a sound, or an image; like the musical elations achieved through Gregorian chant or the Indian *bhajans,* or the rhythmic ecstasies of the Sufi dervishes in Turkey and some African tribes. This concept of getting "lost" in a repetitive movement or vocalization certainly dovetails with Dr. Cloninger's self-transcendence scale as well, and the common autistic sense of detachment from one's body and limbs in space is called "proprioception."

- Dr. Newberg also discovered that the deeper his subjects descended into prayer or meditation, the more the brain's frontal lobe and limbic system "awakened." (The limbic system is the threshold of the brain's sensitivities and emotions, and is activated when processing language.) At the same time this was occurring in Newberg's patients, the brain's parietal lobe, which orients one to time and space, grew dimmer. Not surprisingly, current autism research is also focusing on these three regions of the brain: the frontal lobe, limbic system, and parietal lobe. In fact, at the University of California San Diego, Dr. Eric Courchesne's MRI-imaging, conducted in ongoing research of brain regions implicated in autism, showed the *loss* of parietal lobe tissue in many individuals with autism—implicating the natural propensity to already be "lost" in space and time or possess an inability to distinguish between one's own body and being separate from one's body, not unlike the "dim" state achieved by Newberg's subjects.

- Newberg additionally found that meditation increases the brain's serotonin production. (Serotonin is an important "feel good" neurotransmitter that is believed to control sleep, mood, body temperature, regulation of appetite, and some sensory perception.) In *The God Gene*, genetic scientist Dr. Dean Hamer contends that "serotonin affects consciousness in many ways that are connected to self-transcendence and spirituality." Hamer continues, "It is in the limbic-brain system that monoamines [including serotonin] intersect with consciousness." Guess what? Studies done since 1961 have shown that many individuals with autism have *elevated* serotonin levels—another predisposition to altered consciousness. Even as this book was in its final stages of editing, important research came to light out of Vanderbilt Center for Molecular Neuroscience and the Vanderbilt Kennedy Center for Research on Human Development connecting serotonin and autism. In 1961, the estimate was that just 25 percent of persons with autism had elevated serotonin, but at that time autism was considered rare. It is now believed that at least half of those with autism also have high serotonin. In his studies, Dr. Newberg found that those neuro-typical subjects most likely to be "spiritual" had low serotonin levels as opposed to those with higher levels who may have been religious but needed to "see to believe." However, this indicates a deliberate choosing of beliefs, and I am suggesting that—where autism is concerned— it makes no difference as such folks are *naturally* spiritual and have no reason to question what they experience.

- Also in *The God Gene*, Dr. Hamer discusses the capacity for altered consciousness stemming from a common form of epilepsy in the brain's temporal lobe that impacts the limbic system. During the subtle, sometimes-undetectable seizures—which have historically had spiritual implications for some—dreamlike hallucinations are commonplace. A 2002 study published in *Brain* magazine explored seizure activity in children with Tuberous Sclerosis Complex (TSC), which is associated with autism. One conclusion of the study demonstrated "a possible link between temporal lobe epilepsy and the development of an autism spectrum disorder in children with TSC." Additionally, a 2002 Penn State College of Medicine study, "A Review of Current Thoughts on Localized Structural Lesions in Autistic Disorder," similarly concluded, "The temporal region dysfunction may be implicated in almost all of the clinical symptoms in autism (perceptive, emotional, and cognitive deficits), since these associative regions are highly connected with the frontal and parietal lobes and the limbic and associated sensory systems." This corresponds autism research with Newberg and Hamer's work.

- Parents and caregivers know that food is usually extremely important to their loved ones; eating is one of the few pleasures engaging *all the senses* in which the person with autism can revel on a daily basis. Some would even say their loved one is absolutely passionate about eating. As serotonin affects appetite, serotonin production can *increase* through eating, especially sweets. (How many of us know someone with autism who has devoured an entire chocolate cake left unattended on a kitchen counter?) Do such individuals with autism naturally create elevated serotonin levels, in part, through their diet, thus feeding their spirituality? More than nourishment, food affirms our humanity and our joy of being alive. Andrew from Ontario, Canada, spoke of his autistic communion, "It is a spiritual experience to prepare and eat a meal with friends."

• Finally, in *The God Gene*, Dr. Hamer presents his research in isolating at least one gene, labeled VMAT2, which he identifies as a DNA marker for spirituality. Hamer identified VMAT2 as having the "greatest effect on the overall self-transcendence scale and...the self-forgetfulness scale." It should not be surprising to learn that VMAT2 controls the flow of monoamines (including serotonin) in the brain, "brain chemicals that play a key role in emotions and consciousness," Hamer summarizes. A report in the August 2005 *American Journal of Human Genetics* has already shown an association with autism and another serotonin-related gene called SERT. It will be fascinating to see if VMAT2 has a role in future genetic research for autism.

Brian, a man with autism from Canada, provided intimate insight with regard to the concept of self-transcendence, as referenced in the work of Doctors Cloninger and Hamer:

I just could not understand, for the life of me, why anyone would want, in any way, to compete with others (such as in sports, card games, political campaigns, job advancements, etc.). Instead, I found myself in the wilds (and I was fortunate to live near the edge of a fairly large city in southwestern Ontario) where I could follow the streams, feel a "rapport" with many of the individual trees, and have strong images of the landscape pressed into my memory for future tributes to a non-competitive life—something that was denied outright or negated then and is still treated with repulsion these days.

When I was in these natural areas, I often felt a deep sense of spirituality, of a "presence" that I could not explain to myself or others; it was as if I was being drawn to that place at that moment just to feel what "being" was all about. I felt a commonality with everything that I saw, heard, smelt, and touched at that moment and did not want to let go of it as I realized that it would be next to impossible to explain the depth of feeling that I had, then and there, to others (especially those who propagated the competitive spirit). There was no competition, per se, at all, during these "divine" moments (if I may call them that), and it was as though I was receiving something beyond any "knowledge"…something that was telling me that I, nor others, did not need to "compete" in order to feel the Divine Will in the order of time. This Divine Will was there, right before me, as long as I was alone and put aside any need to be with other people. Loneliness was not a lack of being with people; it was a lack of being able to explain, in any way, these moments to others in my life...I am constantly being told [by clergy] that despite any such experiences, those who want to worship God must gather together, and that God has commanded His people to worship Him. When I challenge them to the need for "physically" gathering together (as I see myself being "gathered together" spiritually with many others during those "divine experiences"), they dismiss my statements as "out of context" to the "true meaning" of "God's will." But this only drives me further away from the clergy and more into these personal experiences with God.

Dr. Harold Koenig, psychologist and codirector of the Center for Spirituality, Theology, and Health at Duke University, echoes these sentiments in his research, going so far as suggesting that spirituality is an antidote to depression. "Generally, religious people have a positive view of the world," said Koenig. "They believe they are here for a reason. They see a purpose and meaning in their life and have hope...They feel that God is with them and gives them strength." Dr. Koenig's observations lend credence for those with autism when someone like Matthew communicates, "I am a man. For a long time I was treated as a child. I run to God when I am weak. He says I am strong."

Science and research aside, among the typical population some people remain solid in their spiritual faith because of core beliefs instilled from upbringing. Others find their faith as the result of a life-altering event, personal tragedy, or great loss. But Heidi, a professional from Ohio, became spiritually detached as a byproduct of witnessing abuses committed against persons with autism and others. She is in the process of rediscovering her faith, and reflected:

> I have worked in the mental retardation/developmental disabilities field twenty-one years now, and I have seen how terribly people with disabilities have been treated. Part of my not believing in God has come from seeing abuse happen and not much done about it. All of this also added to my non-belief, but under the surface I have always felt there was more going on than most people are sensitive to. One of my toughest cases ever was a young man with autism who had such severe self-injurious behavior he was restrained 100 percent of the time; he also screamed nonstop. From the first day I met him, he became one of the special people in my life, and every time he sees me he immediately looks deep into my eyes, and then responds with a smile. While I justified his situation with seeing this as proof that there is no God, I always knew he knew otherwise...[I] have really opened up to seeing that some terrible things happen, not because there is no God or that God has forsaken them, but that maybe if there is a Higher Being, the bad stuff is allowed to happen to those who become better people from it.

I, too, once shared Heidi's spiritual angst and, just as well, attributed it to the abuses *I* received: daily verbal abuse, routine physical abuse, and public humiliations in the form of mocking my passions, my speech, or my body language. I developed a bitter, caustic edge tinged with snobbery. It provoked me to make sarcastic, cynical remarks, or hurtful jokes at the expense of others. My humor was maudlin and morose, often about injury or death. I sought to inflict pain to deflect from my own unresolved issues of self-acceptance. Inside, I felt cold and gray, hard and ugly—and I felt justified. I was not completely absent of compassion, but its remote glimmers were spotty and dull.

Approaching middle age, I was still without the framework of Asperger's Syndrome to provide a rationale for my life; this did not happen until I befriended those with autism, in whom I could identify similar traits. Instead, I was blaming of myself, my personal quirks and idiosyncrasies, and my inability to blend socially. In the midst of this I became depressed as I was wont to do since my teen years. I disregarded the symptoms of irritability, fatigue, and the feeling that *everything* required such great effort so that it was exhausting to get through each day. Because I wasn't attuned to myself and what my body was telling me, I received the first of many wake-up calls that made it loud and clear: pay attention, take stock of who you are, and trust your inner knowing.

In spring 1999, I was driving home from an errand, my mind on other things, and realized I had just missed my exit off the highway. I was still within driving distance to reach it, and I impulsively crossed the median strip that divided the roads. As I did, I sideswiped another car to my right. Instinctively, I slammed on the brakes and pulled back onto the median strip. The other driver had pulled off the highway as well, and I darted out between traffic to approach her.

Upon reaching the other car, I discovered a badly-shaken elderly woman who was more upset than I. The length of her car's driver side was totaled: crushed and terribly scarred. She was, fortunately, unhurt and most gracious and forgiving, telling me accidents happen. I quickly learned that she had just dropped her husband off at the hospital for triple-bypass surgery. A car accident was the absolute last thing she needed! I felt awful! It was my fault for not paying attention—where all things were concerned. I was so upset and concerned for her that the extent of damage to my car hadn't entered my mind until I was sure she was okay.

As I stepped away and turned toward my car, I was stunned. I could see *no* damage! I couldn't believe it! I saw nothing; no point of impact that made the god-awful *whump!* as the cars collided. After we exchanged insurance information and the woman drove away, I did finally notice a few minor scrapes on the edge of the passenger side rear view mirror—the object of hindsight and self-reflection. The glass there had shattered, but that was all. To attain atonement, I had to "reflect" by shedding all pretenses and assuming a position of abject humility. It was one in a series of spiritual lessons to come, one catalyst that contributed to a shift.

Many parents and caregivers of children with autism already recognize the blessings their children offer on many levels; for them, spiritual conviction didn't derive from a catastrophe or accident of any kind. It was introduced or strengthened by virtue of their child *being* in their lives. A 2003 research project conducted by Tanisha Rose, a psychology student at Lincoln University in Philadelphia, examined the stress levels among parents of children with autism. One of Rose's four hypotheses was that as the importance of religion increased, the level of stress experienced by parents would decrease—a factor largely neglected in past stress studies. Rose's study indicated that parents with elevated stress shared a lack of positive religious practices.

As I've noted, I'm not suggesting that *all* persons with autism are spiritually gifted; my ability to discern this is logistically impossible! And so, by reading this, you may be unable to surmise anything in particular that might be described as spiritually gifted or unique about your own loved one (at least on the levels about which I've speculated). Stuart from New Jersey, dad to teenaged Spencer, wrote:

> He does seem to have an appreciation of nature, especially large bodies of water. This he seems to share with me...Although he doesn't have an innate spiritual or religious sense, he does, however, possess one of the most developed moral perspectives that I have ever encountered. He has a profound sense of right and wrong, especially with regard to sexuality and relationships. I must add, though, that he seems extremely detached from his spiritual side and is a bit atheistic.

SPIRITUALITY AT WORK

Is spirituality at work even in such instances? The beauty in this concept is found in its simplicity. It *is* there, it's simply showing itself subtly, quietly, and over time. Of course your loved one does not have to be party to some inspired event—such as those documented in this work—in order for you to so deeply love and appreciate her; you love and appreciate her exactly for who she is, not *what* she is. The spirituality shows through daily, in all the little ways that no one ever considered, like the mother driving with her daughter through snow-covered scenery. The little girl with autism, taking it all in, remarked in awe that the landscape looked just like powdered sugar and indeed it did—a perspective her mother would never have otherwise considered and now cherishes.

In other ways, everyday spirituality comes through in how the person with autism determines the best way to get his needs met without the support or assistance of anyone else's wisdom or professional expertise. It's these ingenious moments of independently discovered modes of coping that may prompt you to wonder how in the world he figured it out alone!

Bill was widowed in fall 2003 and, as the father of two children, he was naturally concerned for his youngest, Chris, a brilliant nine-year-old boy with autism. Bill wrote:

> My wife was only a few days from death; her body was shutting down. She was sleeping, but she looked up at me and said, "You're a good man Bill. I worry about you. I don't worry about Chris. He is very strong. Find someone nice for him." I assured her that I would always love her and take care of the kids.

And so it has played out that in just over a year since his mother's passing, Chris has rapidly grown and become increasingly independent. As Bill observed, "Chris has proven to be the strongest of us all." He continued:

> Chris asked me to stop all supplements and medicines, and has demanded his own time and independence. This has allowed me to take back my life a little. Chris has given me faith and vision. Chris has taught me what love and life is all about. He is my heart. My wife still continues to guide me. We miss her…we ache for her.

Chris has historically been a man of few words, though he struggles persistently to make his vocalizations understood by all. In particular, he was challenged in articulating the word water so that it sounded like WA-TER. Reaching the pinnacle of impatience with his teachers one day, Chris reached for his communication device and, by himself, typed out "AQUAFI-NA"—a perfectly acceptable alternative that meant the same thing and gratified his needs (shades of his mom's sarcasm, said Bill).

Isn't it plausible that the person with autism comes into the lives of the parents who need him most, deliberately and by supreme design? Deirdre is the mother of a wonderful nine-year-old son who, by her definition, "happens to be diagnosed with Asperger's Syndrome." Deirdre hasn't seen that her son outwardly demonstrates any particular spiritual giftedness, although she reports that recently he is beginning to become questioning and inquisitive about God, Heaven, and human mortality. For Deirdre, the gifts her son offers simply by being in her life have developed into a personal appreciation of others. She continued remarking about her son:

> The road to discovering what makes him different was difficult. He was not like other children, we knew that. But coming to the understanding that he's neurologically different and not just willfully stubborn and resistant opened up new possibilities for us. His diagnosis gave us a pathway for learning how to help him make his way through his world.
>
> A side benefit of this realization came to me slowly. My son's diagnosis has made it possible for *me* to make my way through *my* world and look at it through a different prism. I'm less likely to be judgmental of people I encounter in everyday life. I'm willing to consider that the abrupt businessman or odd grocery-store clerk might just be struggling with social skills. I think about those people in my life who have been labeled as "brilliant but lazy" or "pompous and rude" and look beyond the labels. I'm more open to looking for the good in those people without automatically being dismissive.
>
> The world is filled with all kinds of people. All of them have strengths and weaknesses. I want people to look at my son and see the beauty and grace within. Wishing that for him has made me look harder at those who are passed over by so many. And my life has been enriched beyond compare.

We should view the anecdotes that follow in succeeding chapters with wonder and awe, not with envy or disappointment because your loved one with autism hasn't had similar experiences. We *all* have the capacity to hold spiritual gifts in order to be of service to others, particularly if we abandon traditional limitations and remain open. Those with such gifts—including persons with autism—usually don't know that there is anything extraordinary about them. These gifts come inherently as a byproduct of being human. As you've read, simply by enacting the three miracles, there is potential for greater reciprocal clarity in our relationships with individuals with autism. Beyond that, the sky's the limit, as echoed by Sharon Marie from Edmonton, Canada, in reflecting upon her own son's Asperger's Syndrome:

> We are truly blessed to have high-functioning autistics in our world. I believe that they are a higher level of being. From their deep sense and connection to the universe and our planet they feel what a leaf feels, they can smell cold, they are truly in the moment. These special beings can teach us many things through their gifts that they have to offer. The creativity and intelligence of people with Asperger's Syndrome have led to some of our greatest scientific, technological, and artistic advancements. If only we could open our hearts and minds to celebrate the diversity of these amazing people. Perhaps, then we might find a world of peace like the song "Imagine" by John Lennon.

Let's now continue on our journey by exploring select areas of giftedness in certain individuals with autism as shared by the persons themselves, their parents, and caregivers.

Divine
Experiences

three

Speaking in Silence

‰

When we think of the autistic experience, we most often think of folks who count among their obstacles limitations or challenges in producing verbal speech. Others are not "wired" for speech at all. Our Creator makes no mistakes, and not speaking is simply and naturally the beauty of their design. Few of us know what it is to have the use of our voice regulated or forcibly removed save for a temporary bout of laryngitis or a tonsillectomy.

The late freelance writer Sally Siegel defined her loss of speech, resulting from a stroke, as similar to persons with autism when she wrote, "Now I could not make my simplest wish known, and yet I fully comprehended everything that was going on around me....I also developed a bizarre habit of saying 'yes' when I meant 'no' and all the while being aware of how I was miscommunicating." Though Siegel regained her speech shortly afterwards, she endured intense frustration and humiliating and insensitive treatment from others that left her thoughtful and pensive in her renewed appreciation of those with long-term speech loss. In reflecting upon others, Siegel wrote, "I hope that those who are healthy among us realize the person they loved has not changed. That person is confined within the prison of the body. The spirit is free."

Consider what it might be like if such temporary experiences were prolonged and became a way of life for any one of us, our communication reduced to aping pantomimes in a relentless version of charades. Such is the native tongue of so many with autism. How would we express our basic wants and needs, let alone pain and discomfort? Think too, how much time would be spent in silence or devoted to introspection, contemplation, reflection, and other deep thoughts. Not to mention the frustrating horrors and social injustices endured from those not presuming our intellect. We would suffer those trials for the sake of our soul's education. But there would also be broad blocks of time in which to be absorbingly meditative. Mother Teresa reiterates throughout her writings, "God loves silence." Other spiritual visionaries affirm that the divine is found in the golden silence of our own selves. And Dr. Wayne Dyer teaches, "For it is when you merge into the silence and become one with it that you reconnect to your source and know the peacefulness that some call God."

THE RIGHT TO COMMUNICATE

The absence of speech certainly does not mean that people are without a desire to communicate. The right to communicate is one of the most essential of all human rights. It is *critically urgent* that all alternative modes of communication be exhausted in seeking a "match" or "matches" that best suit each unique individual without a voice. Here are but a few examples of barrier-breaking communication techniques.

- Speech therapy is recommended for anyone who puts forth the effort to articulate language. This is a demonstration of tremendous will in knowing that the world best accommodates those who speak. (Sometimes those who can handwrite will verbalize in unison.) Foster instant engagement through mutually-pleasing activities or by building upon an individual's most passionate topics of interest as the focus of conversation.

- Music is a necessary part of life that heals and soothes. It is a universal language extremely important to so many with autism and may be used to elicit discernable vocalizations through song, in addition to reciprocation in relationships through the active "call" and "response" of its flow.

- Self-expression through art is another universal language. The beauty of color, shape, and form are comprehended by all who create and the recipients who assimilate those creations with their senses.

- Please limit the use of sign language as the *primary* mode of communication to intimate family and friends; it is not universally understood in our communities, but if it is used in the context of the family unit, please preserve it because it works. (Otherwise everyone around the individual has an obligation to maintain consistent fluency or we risk disservicing him.)

- Picture Exchange Communication Systems (PECS) comprise pictures, icons, and words on personal, manageable cards accessible at all times by the user. They communicate a want, need, or desire when an exchange is initiated from the individual to her caregiver. PECS is a lovely foundation, particularly for those so visual, but it is limited to the parameters set for what we *think* someone wishes to communicate.

• Augmentative and Alternative Communication (AAC) has been of good service to many through technology or simple, homemade devices. AAC may include computer programs, pre-programmed products, or small portable word processors. Many have display screens, word-prediction (once the first few letters are indicated), icon-based keyboards, and voice output to enable independent communication. Extraordinary pieces of technology may even be activated via manual switches or with eye gaze or head-pointing.

FACILITATED COMMUNICATION

Facilitated Communication (FC) is another AAC communication method. It is predicated upon safe and trusting relationships and a belief in competence. An individual unable to speak, or with limited or unreliable speech, is physically supported at the hand, wrist, elbow, or shoulder by a loyal communication partner with as much or as little support as is needed. The partner or "facilitator" *does not* guide the person, or make choices for them in this way. Instead, the physical support is a catalyst that trips an internal switch, allowing an individual to tap their confidence and initiate motor-coordination capabilities in order to forcefully touch pictures, icons, words, objects, or a keyboard. (It is also not unusual for verbal speech to come as a result of this "rewiring" process.) Unlike some methods, use of a keyboard to express one's wants and needs, thoughts, feelings, and desires is a *boundless* communication opportunity. FC is not a "cure," rather it allows a person's true individuality to surface while creating strong bonds between the individual and his or her communication partner. We may authenticate an individual's communications as her own when unique or surprising patterns, phrases, or words emerge; words are misspelled, spelled phonetically, or spelled "shorthand" style (you = u); someone refers to themselves in the third person, or by pet names; or we verify what has been communicated as founded in fact.

The veracity of Facilitated Communication has been disputed in the past. Rather than assessing its efficacy on a person-by-person basis, FC's dissenters have issued a uniform moratorium on its use; but because some cancer patients don't respond to chemotherapy doesn't mean we unilaterally withhold it as a treatment option for all the rest. Now numerous studies in peer-reviewed journals have since condoned the method repeatedly and assuredly. The ultimate goal of FC is independence in communication free of any physical support, such as many have achieved. In this way, persons with autism are shattering antiquated perceptions by revealing their true intellect and explaining away misunderstood, stereotypical "behaviors." Jenn is one such person, a young woman passionate about educating others.

> I am so happy to be able to communicate and let my
> thoughts be known, whether I am happy, sad, angry,
> frustrated, or horrified. It was raging frustration all
> the years I was silent. My behavior showed it. Life is
> very different. I don't carry that frustration with me
> anymore. I have my moments, but not weeks of bad
> times.

For years, Jenn was believed to be mentally retarded. She is now a successful college student in her senior year majoring in psychology.

An Internet search for "Augmentative and Alternative Communication" will lead to a number of websites including those of major technology manufacturers. School autistic support staff, special educators, speech-language pathologists, and certain university faculty can be resources for thoroughly exploring any of the preceding communication options, singularly or in combination. It is crucial that the right to communicate be preserved for all persons.

The liberation Facilitated Communication offers is successful for some otherwise unable to articulate speech like those with autism, Parkinson's, Cerebral Palsy, or the aftereffects of stroke. It is often a viable mode for the many people with autism who appear to teach themselves to read at a very early age. Clinically speaking, this precocious proficiency is called hyperlexia. Dr. Douglas Biklen is director of Syracuse University's Facilitated Communication Institute, dean of the university's School of Education, and coproducer of the 2005 Academy Award-nominated short subject *Autism is a World*. As early as 1991, Biklen, who first introduced FC to the

United States, observed, "What we're discovering is that most of the people that we work with already are literate. It's particularly surprising to see these literacy skills in very young children, even three-year-olds." My friend Mark responds to those who would question his ability to read and spell, "I was a sponge and absorbed the world around me. Because I couldn't speak or ask questions, I took everything in and filed it in my brain for future use. I believed that someday I would be able to communicate." To further explain, Matthew, a thirty-six-year-old man, reflected, "I read by keeping my eyes on the page as it goes by me. I read the whole page at a time. You read one sentence at a time."

Izzy attempts to articulate what transpires with his FC communication partners where the mechanics of the process are concerned, "I am not sure of the exact technical details of how to explain this, but I pick up on their heartbeat—this can be done with some people, not with all people—and then I am able to type and communicate." Will, another young man, considers FC very spiritual as well as cerebral: "When I facilitate, I'm exposing my soul. This simple process is intimate and very private; a communion between two people working in tandem." Will types either independently or with a gentle touch at the elbow.

Lori communicates verbally but is at her most eloquent when using Facilitated Communication:

> The special reason I chose this life is I need to teach people about love. People love me because they see me as I am. It is hard for them to love me because I have a problem. I talk bad. I have my best thinking

when I type. Typing makes my thinking stronger. It
helps me organize my thoughts. I love to type.

Devlyn Lighthawk described her spiritual desire to liber-
ate others through Facilitated Communication.

Between the FC supporter and FC communicator
lies the same vast universes of spiritual light, connected
in wonder and intent. Me, I just want to be a bridge,
because I can, to be an FC counselor, one-on-one,
knowing and being in both worlds…stars and the
empty space between…inviting and sharing the gift
of autistic ability.

THE DORMANT LANGUAGE

Telepathy is another mode of expression bonded in intimacy.
Sigmund Freud, preeminent psychiatrist, stated that telepathy is a primitive form of communication made dormant by
language. If, like Sally Siegel, we were all suddenly rendered
mute indefinitely, without any means to communicate, we
would eventually gravitate into little colonies where we'd
instinctively intuit one another's thoughts and feelings without
words. One colleague offers examples of ways we often use a
telepathic "mental push" in our everyday lives. He cites the person who is watching lottery numbers being drawn on television,
has matched the first two of three numbers, and is silently "willing" the third number to appear. Or the football fans that, once
the ball is soaring aloft, attempt to telepathically "push" the ball
toward and through the goalpost uprights. Other, everyday
examples include "mother's intuition"; having a "hunch" or

"gut instinct" that proves accurate; getting good, bad or indifferent "vibes" upon first meeting someone; or knowing when your pet doesn't feel well just by looking at him.

When we think of persons with autism who live in silence, it certainly makes good sense that telepathy is one such mode of communication. We may define telepathy as the ability to mentally communicate thoughts, emotions, words, or images silently to another being with the intent that they will receive, interpret, and act upon those communications. Couldn't that definition also apply to the times we silently send spiritual communications to the Higher Power in which we hold our most precious of all beliefs? This is what we call meditation or prayer. Telepathy should not be so quickly criticized when many of us practice it daily in this way. Don't we pray in the belief that the Universe will hear our prayers and act upon them? If we didn't believe in the power of prayer, we'd surely cease doing it. And if God created us as individual, unique, and natural works of art in His image, it is conceivable that we all have the capacity to silently communicate with both Him *and* with one another.

Jennifer, a caseworker from northern Pennsylvania, described her experience with this very concept upon meeting one gentle young man:

> Sid and I met for the first time at his Individualized Education Plan meeting. I had never met a person diagnosed with Childhood Disintegrative Disorder [an experience on the autism spectrum] before and wasn't sure what to expect. Sid is fifteen years old and quite tall. When I first saw him, he was sitting

alone working on a puzzle. His teacher asked him if he wanted to go to his meeting. Sid stood up and went to the corner of the room. He stood there for a few moments staring at me. Then, deciding that he would go to his meeting, he proceeded towards the classroom door while maintaining his gaze on me, and left the room. I followed Sid and introduced myself. Sid said, "Hello Jennifer" and lead me to the library where the meeting would take place.

During the meeting, Sid and I sat at opposite ends of the table and began to engage in our own inter-action. I started to think, or wonder, what Sid thought about this meeting. What did he really think? Did he like his teachers? Was this boring for Sid?

I decided that maybe Sid could hear me without words. Why not? I asked Sid, or rather *thought to* Sid, "Is this boring for you? What do you think of these meetings?" Sid *did* react. He smiled, looked at me, and then began to laugh and laugh. Something was funny.

I wasn't sure; that was probably coincidence, but I had to ask Sid. I thought, "Sid, if you can actually hear me, touch your right hand with your pencil." Again Sid reacted by looking at me and touching his right hand with his pencil.

This was interesting, but it could have still been coincidence. I couldn't think of anything else to ask. However, I did start thinking about Sid and his family being new to the area and the ties they have already established in their new town. For some reason, I started to think about Christmas and the church and school activities during that time of year. I wondered what the holiday would be like for them this year. Sid started singing "O Christmas Tree" and was drawing and decorating a Christmas tree in his notebook. I really wasn't surprised.

Someday this summer, I hope to spend more time with Sid and "talk" with him. Sid is considered "non-verbal." I just don't think people are listening.

While many of our loved ones with autism may be blessed with the gift of telepathy, they may not yet fully comprehend it. A gentle and loving caregiver will need to explain it. Think on this: as a child, I was blessed with an inordinate artistic talent. It was some time before I came to understand—from the cumulative effect of others "oohing" and "ahhing" in awe—that this was not so for everyone. I didn't think I was doing anything differently than anyone else. Similarly, as a person with Asperger's Syndrome, I "think" in constant streams of mental, visual imagery: pictures and movies. I assumed this was typical of how *everyone* thinks. I still grapple with what I've only come to learn in the past few years: that it is rare for others to think in so effortlessly and fluently a manner. Children and animals, as the purest of innocents, often perceive spiritual experiences only because they haven't yet been conditioned *not to*. Remember this, then, when applying the concept to others. The person with autism may simply not be fully cognizant of her very special gift, and may assume that *everyone* communicates in this way. This is an autistic way of thinking.

COMPASSIONATE ACCOMMODATION

Many folks with an autistic experience are extremely visual in their comprehension and retention of information. It is important to communicate information to them without relying exclusively upon verbal speech, which is the preferred communication of most neuro-typical people. For the person who thinks in pictures, our words *dissipate* into thin air right after we've said them. They are not tangible. Nor do they linger so that the person may refer to them as they hang in the air. Most people with autism will require visuals to reinforce spoken concepts and make them concrete. This is best accomplished through a simple written or pictorial story that becomes that person's property. The story is *visually* reviewed with her as often as is needed until it becomes second nature. She will best assimilate and retain the information in this manner. With gentle prompts and reminders, she may then acknowledge her understanding through practical application of the concept. It may also be helpful if the person is given the opportunity to illustrate the story herself in order to personalize it. (For those who are more auditory than visual, this and other stories may be tape recorded and replayed.)

Here is a sample story explaining telepathy, which may be modified to suit your needs.

My Gift

God [or synonym for Higher Power] created me as a beautiful human being.
When God creates human beings, He blesses us each with gifts.

The gifts are like presents but we can't hold them or unwrap them.

Instead, the gifts are part of who we are, like our eye color or the color of our skin.

The gifts are with us all the time.

Gifts may also be called talents.

I may know someone who has a gift for singing beautifully or playing a musical instrument.

Or I may know someone who draws beautifully or plays a sport really well.

People may call them talented because of what they do.

I have gifts too.

Some of them may include _____.

One of my gifts is that I may sometimes know or see what others are thinking.

I may sometimes know or see what others are feeling too.

I may do this without anyone telling or showing me. I just know it.

If I choose to, I will tell these things to people I love and trust like _____.

Other people may not know or see what others are thinking and feeling like I do.

They may not be able to tell these things about me either.

I need to find other ways to tell them what I am

> thinking and feeling.
>
> I will try to do this by (list all the ways in which this individual can communicate that are effective, reliable, and universally understandable)_____
>
> _____.
>
> When I do this, people will be able to better understand me.

If any such experiences are causing your loved one with autism to become agitated, distressed, and derailed to the point of being unable to focus on daily routines, it is advisable that you also seek professional counseling to rule out any mental health issues, such as acute anxiety, that may be exacerbating what someone is experiencing. This precaution does not undermine the validity of those experiences, it is simply an additional and responsible support.

Donna Williams, a bestselling author and prominent autism self-advocate, broaches an interesting nuance of telepathy that must be considered. She writes in her book, *Nobody Nowhere*:

> At school strange things were happening. I would have daydreams in which I was watching children I knew. I would see them doing the most trivial things: peeling potatoes over the sink, getting themselves a peanut butter sandwich before going to bed. Such daydreams were like films in which I'd see a sequence of everyday events that really didn't relate in any way to myself. I began to test the truth of these daydreams, approaching the friends I'd seen in them and

asking them to give a step-by-step detailed picture of what they were doing at the time I had the daydream. Amazingly, to the finest detail, I would find I had been right. This was nothing I controlled, it simply came into my head, but it frightened me.

The exquisitely sensitive individual may *be* aware of the unusual nature of her gift. It may seriously unnerve her, though, when it is realized that others do not typically have such visions. It will be very important that those who know, love, and care for her best are in the position of providing patient, loving, and gentle counsel about the gift. The caregiver may reinforce that it was bestowed from God or a Higher Power and that, while unique, is not something to dread.

Rebecca is a Maryland mom who shared one instance about the urgent timeliness of her daughter Katie's unspoken communication.

It was 6:30 p.m. on a Tuesday night. Myself along with about eight of my friends routinely gathered every Tuesday to work on a community project. Our goal was to raise money for a large playground for our kids. We chose to bring all of our children so they could play together in my backyard on our play set. We purchased one of those large clubhouse swing sets. We decided to have it placed strategically facing the kitchen windows to allow us to keep an eye on the children from inside the house. This play set is one of those that has a banister up ten steps with a front porch in front of the clubhouse. It had a regular door that opened and closed and also shutters that covered over the windows. Underneath the clubhouse was a very large sandbox. The kids loved to come to our house to play.

At about 6:45 I was preparing hot tea for some of my friends. To this day, I cannot explain what exactly happened. I had a rush that completely encompassed my entire body. And something was drawing me to the window. My teacup fell and broke into slivers. My heart racing, I looked out the window to find that my youngest daughter was missing. The rest of the children were on the swings, on the seesaw, and on the monkey bars, but Katie was nowhere to be found. The door to the clubhouse was closed. The shutters over the windows were closed. She was in there and I knew it, but I also knew that something absolutely horrible was happening. I raced out of my house and dashed up the stairs to find Katie in the lap of a fourteen-year-old neighborhood boy. Her pants were pulled down and so were his.

As a mother, words cannot describe what went through my mind and my heart. I held my baby and demanded that he leave my yard and never return.

My daughter was three years old then, and has been diagnosed with severe mental retardation and autism. She could not speak at all outside of sounds and noises. Did she somehow cry out for me without a voice? Was it mother's intuition? I guess I'll never know. Whatever it was, I thank God that I heard her in time.

ANIMALSPEAK

Francis of Assisi was celebrated in the thirteenth century for his intuitive aptitude of communicating with the animal kingdom, creatures of all shapes and sizes including wolves, birds, even fish. In addition to telepathy with other people, it is common that some with autism communicate similarly with animals. Patrick is a fourteen-year-old boy living in rural Pennsylvania. His family tends two horses in addition to other animals. Patrick's mother, Doreen, related that he demonstrated a strong, unspoken connection with animals at an early age. Doreen wrote:

> We bought a mare quarter horse named Jesse six years ago. She was five years old. I remember that because Jesse and Kara [Patrick's younger sister] are the exact same age. Jesse had been abused. You couldn't get near her head, and she was terrified of lead rope. Also, she had been with cows and not with other horses. Jesse is unlike other horses. She is not a social animal. She could care less about being around other horses. It's okay for her to be alone.
>
> We got Jesse and she ran from us because she was afraid and very fearful. So we asked the woman from whom we had purchased Jesse what to do. She said to tie Jesse in the barn for three days and just go down every couple of hours with a treat, such as an apple or a carrot to let her get used to us and let her know we were going to bring her food and not harm her. Even after days of this, and Jesse getting used to us and her new home, she still would not let us touch

her head. One time, I tried to put her in the stall to feed her and she reared and my hand was all cut up from her rearing and from me trying to grab the lead rope.

I called the women again and asked, "What's wrong with this horse?" She didn't know what had happened to her; you just couldn't get near this horse. You couldn't wave your arms or lift your arms in any way without this horse freaking out. So what we did was we got Jesse tied in the stall again. Then we would just go down and wave our arms. Her eyes would become white with fear and she would jerk at the rope. Finally she got used to us just coming in and knowing we wouldn't harm her. But she could not get use to us waving our arms.

We'd probably had Jesse less than one month when Patrick crawled through the fence into the field where we kept the horse. He wasn't used to any horses being in there. He saw no problem crawling through the fence. He was in the field with a fly swatter waving his arms, which should have freaked Jesse out. She should have charged him, but instead, I noticed, she came up to him. I was trying to get to Patrick before the horse did, and I noticed she came up to Patrick. She was watching him calmly. She nuzzled him from behind on his shoulder as if to say, "I am here." If Dan [Patrick's dad], Kara, or I had been doing that, Jesse would have freaked out. But she was calm with Patrick.

We noticed that when Patrick would sit on Jesse, he would become excited. He would make noises and he wouldn't keep his legs still. His legs would move back and forth. His hands would move back and forth. He'd pull at Jesse's mane. He would touch her neck in places that she didn't like to be touched. We also noticed that Jesse remained calm. She would not go ballistic. Her eyes would not become white with fear. She remained calm.

In fact, one Sunday afternoon, for the Hoofbeats Horse Show, Patrick was very agitated. He did not want to participate in the class. He could not wait to get out of the ring. He was on Jesse. He was so mad. He just wanted off. He kept fidgeting and wouldn't hold still for the judging. Jesse was so calm that she actually fell asleep. Patrick is crying, kicking, biting his fingers, totally frustrated, but the horse is so calm. She knows that Patrick is on her. She fell asleep. At other horse shows, where Kara has ridden Jesse, if a horse or somebody makes a sudden move, Jesse is ready to jump out of her skin. She can't tolerate it. She's a very nervous horse, very fearful. We notice the white around her eyes. She's terrified about her situation. However, when Patrick is around her or is riding her, she seems very calm. It's like she understands Patrick. She's been a very good horse with Patrick. I have no explanation why Jesse is so calm with my son and why, with Kara, she's very nervous.

Patrick has always been the subject of animals' attention. It basically was unwanted attention at first. He does not like animals that he doesn't know. When strange dogs or stray cats would come here, or we would go somewhere where they would have an animal, they would always go to Patrick first. He would display fear. Instead of the animal showing aggression, which they normally do when someone shows fear toward an animal, they remain calm. They claim that you have to bond with your dogs for you to have a relationship with them. Patrick has never bonded with our dogs, Missy and Rex.

In the summertime, Patrick loves to be outside. It's very common for us to sit on the first step of our kitchen porch. Patrick would sit there while I put his tennis shoes on. The dogs know that Patrick is sitting there. He's kind of "trapped" while I put his shoes on. The dogs come up and give him kisses and wag their tails. They are pushing each other out of the way so they can give Patrick attention, which is another oddity. They say that if you don't pay attention to a dog, pet it, and befriend it, it's not going to pay any attention to you. Patrick hasn't gone out of his way to pet these animals or befriend them. When he is there sitting on the steps they come up to him and they lick him. It's like, "I'm here. Give me attention now." They are so happy to see him. They can give him kisses because he's "trapped" by Mom. His reaction is to giggle and laugh which gets all the more tail wagging and kisses.

There was a time a neighbor called about some stray dogs in the neighborhood. They had snapped at one of his grandchildren and were now in our yard! I went outside to rescue Patrick from these dogs, and to bring him inside. Patrick was on the swing, and there were these two large dogs sitting beside him! I went to bring him in the house because I didn't want him to get bit by these dogs, but the dogs growled at me—they were protecting my son from me.

I notice when Patrick is on the swing and the neighbor kids are playing in their driveway, which is close to our swing, our German Shepherd, Rex, will go over and sit in the hot sun, not under the shade of the tree. He will sit there facing the neighbor children that are playing with his back to Patrick. He keeps an eye on them so that Patrick is not hurt or harmed in any way.

Our cat also lets Patrick pick her up. She doesn't scratch him, like she does us. Sometimes she will meow her displeasure, but she will not bite, put out her claws, or scratch Patrick. She seems to understand that Patrick is somewhat different from us. She is more tolerant of how he handles her and how he pets her.

It amazes us that an animal can tell that there is something special about Patrick and they behave accordingly. I really wish some adults and other people could recognize that and do the same.

Kristine, Patrick's support aide at home, asked Patrick *how* he communicated with his horse, Jesse. She wrote:

I tried to have him use his letter board. I told him he

could point to "P" for pictures, "W" for words, "O" for other, or "NO" if he did not want to share the information. He just pointed to many letters that made no sense. I then wrote the same answers on a piece of paper and asked him if any were correct. He pointed to the word "Pictures." I assume you can take him at his word. I always do.

Knowing that many folks with autism are visual thinkers and learners, it makes perfect sense that Patrick communicates with animals through the reciprocal infusion of imagery. This doesn't seem any different than not comprehending a foreign language until it's been mastered; I have since had others validate this for me. For example, after I made a presentation about Asperger's Syndrome, a woman who aids a teenage boy with Asperger's shared that he told her he exchanges mental pictures with his beloved horses. Others have laughed at him, but he trusted her enough to confide this secret gift. One mom told me that while her young son danced with abandon on the beach under a setting sun, a row of dolphins appeared just off shore and followed her boy in unison as he leapt and swirled in the sand. I wondered, was the "dance" of picture exchange occurring here too? Autism author and nationally recognized self-advocate, Temple Grandin, explains in detail the likenesses between picture-thinking autistics and picture-thinking creatures in her bestselling book, *Animals in Translation*. Grandin speculates that "Autistic people's frontal lobes almost never work as well as normal people's do, so our brain function ends up being somewhere in between human and animal. We use our animal brains more than normal people do, because we have to. We don't have a choice. *Autistic people are closer to animals than normal people are.*" (Of course in this last statement Grandin is referring to the purity of uncorrupted instincts, impulses, senses, and emotions, *not* intellect; like how both my dog and I will suddenly react to a distant siren that no one else yet hears.)

Of Patrick's relationship with horses, Kristine followed up by adding a footnote:

> One day I got the privilege of seeing Patrick ride Jesse. When he got up on his horse the look that came over his face was beautiful. To me, it was a look that said, "I am in Heaven. What a beautiful place to be." I will never forget that look. It showed to me how valuable and important Jesse is to Patrick. I wish I were an artist. I would paint a picture.
>
> When Patrick and I were at the fair this summer, I asked him what he wanted to see. He spelled "HORSES" on his letter board. I took him to the stables. Patrick quietly walked by each horse. Sometimes he would stop and "rock." He would also tap his chin. To me, it seemed, he was listening to the horse. He didn't stop at all of them, just some. I asked Patrick if he would allow me to take his picture with a horse. He got very upset. I didn't take the picture. We then went to see the llamas. A girl asked Patrick if he would like to pet her llama. He did. I asked him if he would allow me to take his picture with the llama, and he allowed me. After this experience, I felt that

whatever connection Patrick has with horses, it is very personal and extremely private. It is between him and *no one else*! It is special only to him and the horses. I am constantly amazed when I see Patrick with horses.

Another young boy enjoys a similarly sacred and unspoken bond with living creatures. Jack, from Virginia, is six years old and is diagnosed with possible mild autism. His account comes courtesy of his mother Maria.

My son Jack has always had a special affection for cows. He feels very deeply for and about them, and they seem to know. Our local farm park has a few Holsteins that are usually at the back end of the pasture when we arrive. After a few minutes we always encourage him to leave, but Jack insists, "My cows are coming for me." And they always do. They will start to low, and then lumber slowly to him, no matter how many children line the fences.

Once we visited an Audubon farm in Ohio. A very sick calf was penned in the barn. My mother and I commented on how the calf was not long for this world. Jack entered and put his hand through the fence. The weak little calf rose, stumbled to him, and lay down where he could pet her. She sighed continuously, clearly comforted. When he left the barn, Jack went into the pasture full of cattle and just sat down, not near any particular one, just blissful to be there. He still comforts himself with pictures of that visit and asks when we can return.

Butterflies are drawn to him as well. Often in summer I will find him sitting looking at a book or a flower with a butterfly sitting on his shoulder, and butterflies hovering about him as he plays in the sandbox or garden.

Paula from Peoria, Illinois, told of her son Sean's unique association with a wild fawn. She summarized his compassionate sensitivities by sharing, "I know my son has made my life far more spiritual than I could imagine."

I'm the mother of Sean, a nine-and-a-half-year-old autistic boy. My son is the most incredible person. He has a passion for people, animals, and nature. Animals are drawn to him, and he is drawn to them. He is also very spiritual. He has been fascinated by God and the Bible for as far back as I can remember.

Every summer my son is enrolled at camp, which is held outside at a forest park. It is very populated with deer. One day I came to camp to pick him up, and he was near the shelter. I was helping him tie his shoe, when he suddenly said, "Here she comes!" I turned around and running towards me was a small fawn. I was startled and backed away, but he moved towards her and she stopped suddenly in her tracks, and they stared at each other. They were literally only five feet from one another. He crouched down and she began to walk towards him. One of the kids at camp startled her and she ran away, but she kept stopping to look back at my son. The weirdest part was that my other two kids were standing there and immediately recognized, as I did, that she was specifically interested in Sean. He later told us that she had something to tell him. Now whether or not that is true, I don't know. I do know this deer was drawn to my son, as he was to her.

I see this all the time with animals. His brother has also made the connection regarding this and reports seeing the same things. He said that when they feed the ducks at his dad's house or go to a petting farm, the animals surround or follow Sean everywhere.

Fifteen-year-old Brett from southeast Pennsylvania has a strong affinity for both horses and dogs. Butch, the family Black Labrador, is especially protective of him. The dog tolerates Brett's rough handling, like doubling as a pillow for Brett to rest his head, but otherwise snaps at anyone who perpetrates similar offenses. A caregiver's Bichon Frise runs to meet Brett at the bus and showers him with affection but is unmotivated to do the same for anyone else.

Brett has only ever spoken once. It was the last time he saw his mother alive, at age eleven. He said "Bye-bye." Shortly thereafter, he awakened in the middle of the night, sobbing. At the same time in a separate hospital location, she had passed away.

The Gift of Prophecy

Yvonne is a mom from New Jersey. Like Brett, her daughter has the gifted capacity to experience telepathy as well as premonitions. According to Yvonne, Brenda is almost seventeen and has mild autism. Yvonne has known for quite a few years that Brenda has special abilities. She wrote:

> When she was young, she would answer questions before they were asked with no clues given at all to her. For example, one time I was driving and she was in the back seat by herself. It was about 1:00 p.m., and I was thinking about what to make for dinner. Out of the blue, she said, "How about spaghetti?" It was the first time she had done that. Another time, my husband and I were on the top floor of our home, and Brenda was two floors down in the rec room playing. There was no intercom or ducts connecting the floors. John and I discussed whether they might go to the movies and what they could see. He walked down the two flights and before he could say anything, she looked up at him and said, "I don't want to go to the movies. I want to play here." It surprised him tremendously.
>
> Another time, we took her to a well-known doctor who had spent time in the Far East. After about fifteen minutes with her, he turned to us and said, "I normally would never consider asking someone I don't know this question, but is Brenda telepathic? She keeps answering my questions before I've said them."
>
> When she was about twelve, we were spending the Fourth of July with some friends on their boat. We had gotten to the fire works site early so we could get a really good position. Suddenly, Brenda got

upset and told Bill, the captain, "Move back." She continued saying it until he moved far enough back to suit her. She made him move like three or four times, each time he backed up a little more. Finally, she yelled at him, "Move back now." He unhappily complied to keep her calm. Needless to say, we were all amazed that the fire works show never went off because there was a misfiring with the first rocket, and a fire flashed horizontally on the deck sending debris right near where we originally had been. In addition to my family, there were five other people on the boat who witnessed that.

Just a few years later, we were again at the beach with the family who had been with us on the earlier Fourth of July story, and some other people. Brenda, who had been quietly reading, suddenly got upset and starting crying, saying, "There will be fire in the sky outside of Paris. The Concorde will crash and people will die. Don't go on the Concorde." That was on the Sunday before the Concorde crashed that Tuesday. For a while, the people who were with us would call to find out if this airline or that airline was okay to fly. Needless to say, it made a lasting memory for all of us.

Isabelle, also from New Jersey, shared some thoughts about Robby, her young son with an autistic experience:

Things happen when he is there. Answers come to questions, as if out of the blue. He runs away, or

> down a road or hallway, which happens to be the
> one where we find a person or place that answers
> the exact question on our minds. Sometimes, he
> reacts strongly to someone in the room—stranger
> or friend. He may sit on the lap of someone who
> needs it most, for no reason at all. The next day, he
> ignores them. The cat likes to sleep with him but
> [pays no attention] when he is awake.

Sissi and her son, Boone, a gifted five-year-old boy with autism, are from a suburb of Albany, Georgia. Boone is quite adept at creating art with computer graphics, which he began using at eighteen months old. He is passionate about clocks and numbers. In fact, his first words were numbers. He verbally called them out at two-and-a-half without anyone having told him about numbers or their meaning. He is usually accurate in telling time, even without looking at a clock. He can also tell military time though he's only seen a military clock once.

Boone has, on many occasions, created pictures that Sissi interpreted as premonitory of significant world events. For six months prior to the September 11, 2001, terrorist attacks, Boone depicted a series of over one hundred clocks set to the time, 9:11. In addition, he drew a fireball in the sky over a wooded area, and smoke billowing from tall buildings with many windows.

Sissi said she's been severely criticized for suggesting such interpretations. But who better to openly interpret Boone's work than the person who loves and knows him best? My respectful speculation is that Boone receives information in the form of mental impressions, or pictures, from Divine Authority. Without command of spoken language and limited to images accessible by computer, Boone does his best to create a "message" or communication through a collage of images that come closest to matching those in his mind.

Sissi also shared the following anecdotes:

> Boone drew "bruises" on his arm with a purple magic marker. He went around for several days nursing these "wounds." I thought he was doing it because he was trying to get attention or understand injuries or something like that. I had no idea what he was really doing.
>
> My mother arrived from South Carolina one day while this was going on. She was wearing a long-sleeved sweater. Boone loves his grandmother very much. He ran up to her and instead of hugging her as he usually does, he said "Oh, poor boo-boo" and pulled her sleeve back. She had a large purple bruise on her elbow in the same spot where Boone had drawn his. He showed her his boo-boo, too. We were stunned to say the least.
>
> Another time we were traveling to Atlanta. Boone began crying, throwing a fit and insisting we stop. We decided to stop for lunch even though we'd only been on the road for an hour. We stopped at a McDonald's with a play park and spent about forty-five minutes there.
>
> When we got back on the road, we hadn't gone more than one exit when we came upon a huge

traffic accident. There were many cars involved and they were towing the badly damaged cars away. I suppose we would have been in the middle of it if Boone hadn't insisted we stop.

Like Boone, Teresa's son, Max, was particularly sensitive to his grandmother's pain and discomfort. Teresa wrote from Bethlehem, Pennsylvania:

Our family took a vacation in August 2004, just before school started. We took my mother with us to Disneyland. We had a great time but when leaving the park, someone bumped my mother and knocked her down to the ground. She ended up with a broken arm. Her arm took six to eight weeks to heal and often when we would see her, Max would ask her if her arm was better yet.

About six weeks into her recovery, she still was not driving. On my way home I called her on my cell phone and asked if she needed anything at the store. She told me what she needed and also asked if I would pick up some aspirin for her arm. After eating, Max and I went to the drugstore. We stopped at my mother's house on the way to see if she needed anything else. Both she and I had forgotten about the aspirin. She didn't remind me, and I had forgotten it. So it was never discussed in front of Max.

Upon reaching the drug store, Max and I went in. He came along to pick out a snack for himself. I went down the aisle where the snacks were but when I turned around, Max was not beside me. I turned around to try and find him. He had disappeared down the aisle next to me. As I turned the corner, he came walking towards me with a bottle of Advil in his hand. He handed it to me and said "Grammy needs these." Stunned that he thought of what I had forgotten, I told him, "Grammy doesn't take Advil, she takes Tylenol." He returned to the display and handed me a box of Tylenol.

We paid for our things and stopped back at my mother's to drop off her items. When she saw the Tylenol, she said, "Thank goodness you remembered!" I told her I hadn't, Max had. I asked her if she had told him when I wasn't looking and she said no. She admitted she also had forgotten. Max was not quite six when this happened.

The person most likely to be unsettled by communications of premonition is the message bearer himself. Such "infused knowledge" is believed to be the fruit of special intervention by the Creator. As was true of the individual with telepathy, the person with the gift of premonition needs exquisitely patient, sensitive support in comprehending his blessing. As before, if your loved one's experiences are causing marked distress and heightened anxiety that create serious obstacles in routines of daily life, please assume a two-pronged approach of support by also seeking mental health counseling. There is tremendous potential for the person with autism to constantly internalize and visually "replay" instances that incite guilt. The person may berate himself or hold himself personally accountable for the tragic occurrences that he foretold. A variation on the previous story may be helpful to that end.

My Gift

God [or synonym for Higher Power] created me as a beautiful human being.
When God creates human beings, He blesses us each with gifts.
The gifts are like presents but we can't hold them or unwrap them.
Instead, the gifts are part of who we are, like our eye color or the color of our skin.
The gifts are with us all the time.

Gifts may also be called talents.
I may know someone who has a gift for singing beautifully, or playing a musical instrument.
Or I may know someone who draws beautifully or plays a sport really well.
People may call them talented because of what they do.

I have gifts too.
Some of them may include _____.
One of my gifts is that I may sometimes see things before they happen.
I may do this without anyone telling or showing me.

I just know it.

Sometimes the things I see may be people getting hurt.

This may be scary or upsetting.

I do not cause harmful things like this to happen on purpose.

It is not my fault.

I only see it and that's okay.

When I see things before they happen, I will tell these things to people I love and trust like _____.

I will try to do this by (list all the ways in which this individual can communicate that are effective, reliable and universally understandable)_____

_____.

When I do this, people will be able to understand me and help me feel better.

EMERGING AND EVOLVING

Like the persons profiled here, I, too, began to recapture some of the same sensations I once had in childhood. The more I connected to individuals with autism and their families, the more I began to feel a sense of total acceptance. I was unconditionally welcomed into their homes. Still others told me I was like one of their own. This kinship derived from my willingness to share my story, to reveal my own humanity, warts and all. When I applied my personal history to the work it never failed to ring true. And if I shared my life story publicly, people would approach me with bewilderment to say, "How could you know so much about my son?" Because of this, a transformation began to unfurl, and I started to emerge from my self-imposed sequestration.

My mood lightened, and I no longer held sunny days in contempt. As I opened myself more to others, some of my awkward traits diminished and remnants of my former self fell away in bitter shards. Not everyone conspired to undermine me. It was okay to greet strangers with a smile instead of a fixed gaze or protective scowl. Subtle laughter came easier. Now babies and small children turned to look at me full in the face and make direct eye contact, to which I smiled and tried to communicate with them silently in return. (One toddler who hadn't seen me in six months physically twisted out of the arms of a caregiver and stretched to reach me just upon hearing my voice.) This was progress for the man who, as a boy, watched in disbelief at the running, laughing children on the recess playground, stunned and confused by their camaraderie.

Synchronicities or "coincidences" flooded back with greater frequency than ever before. (I have come to refer to these instances as "alignments," little guideposts to let us know we're doing precisely what we should be in the moment, all according to plan.) These included those times that I called, emailed, or thought of someone only to have them say they were just about to contact me in the same moment. Take the time I noted an item in an Internet auction that I knew a distant acquaintance was seeking. I emailed him the link to the item and was surprised to receive his reply immediately—he was already online. What he wrote was that, within the past thirty seconds, he had seen the same item and was wondering if I was going to direct him to it. What made this especially remarkable is that our exchange took place at 3:30 a.m.! If you pay careful attention, you may be surprised at how often such "alignments" occur around your loved one with autism, or even yourself.

In another example, a young client with Asperger's Syndrome, passionate about *Gone with the Wind*, asked me if I knew the actor's name that portrayed Scarlett O'Hara's father. Confessing I couldn't recall, I pledged to tell him when we next met. With best intentions, I forgot until the day before our meeting. I was rereading an unrelated book purchased fourteen years earlier and came across an uncanny reference to the inner workings of subconscious memory. It read, "Think of the time that you…were going half mad because you couldn't remember the name of the actor who played Gerald O'Hara in *Gone with the Wind*." There in black and white was the answer: Thomas Mitchell. As soon as I read it, I recalled it from the first reading, though just as easily, I could've looked it up on any *Gone with the Wind* website.

The synchronicities were benign enough. What I did in the moment "clicked," aligned, and segued seamlessly into the next part of my day. Like when I departed the library wishing they had another book by a favored author and, passing a special "new books" shelf, found her latest. Or, I saw a neighbor during a walk and silently thought to myself, "She's pregnant." Two seconds later, I overheard her say she's due in six months. I often desired to complete an activity, leave home, or return from a trip at a set time, and was able to do just that—to the *exact* minute. (Recently, I hoped to start home from a business trip by 6:30 p.m. Not only was I able to leave at that exact minute, I arrived home *precisely* three hours later from a drive that, despite rain, road construction, and a darkening sky, typically took a good fifteen to twenty minutes *longer*.) Before long, however, these amusing curiosities shifted from fluff to fate.

One day I received an email outline of a new model for supporting children with autism. The outline was a daily schedule that appealed to me because it valued children as unique individuals and promoted respectful support in natural, non-segregated environments. I had one reservation though. Nowhere did I see opportunities for "downtime" within the schedule or opportunities for kids to self-advocate this need (I refer to this in my other books as the "social out").

Blending at recess, engaging with group interactions, or "play" activities one-on-one is *work* for someone with an autistic experience. This is why kids come home from school and totally melt down, prompting teachers to say, "But she's fine during the day!" Parents are often left to feel like it's their fault, somehow. Kids who "hold it together" during the day and then melt down at home have a tremendous, unrecognized *strength*. They realize the social expectation that they "pass," get by, and fit in all day long with *no* breaks or downtime. This is not helpful when we consider how we *all* pace ourselves through bathroom, cigarette and coffee breaks, water cooler conversations, or lunch hour walks.

I forwarded the new outline along with a statement of my cautions to an email list of friends and colleagues. I got to one name on the list and neither recognized the person nor the email address. I almost didn't include that address in my mailing, but on second thought, I recanted and sent the message anyway. A couple hours later I heard back from that very person with grateful thanks. It was the mother of a teenager for whom I had consulted some months back. The very experience I've described had *just* occurred for him at school that week, leading her to nearly hospitalize him because of his reactions. Upon her investigation, it turned out he had very legitimate reasons for being so upset.

On another occasion, I received an "impression," or mental image, of another teenage boy with Asperger's Syndrome with whom I had once consulted. In following up, his parents indicated he was fine but focused increasingly on desiring to develop friendships and be accepted. A month later, they noticed symptoms of depression. The symptoms could be traced back in time concurrent with my initial impression.

Likewise, when consulting for a silent young man in his twenties, I felt that he had once been burned by hot water. I was told this was unlikely because there was no reference to such an incident in his data. Several weeks later, I received a phone call telling me that a more thorough record review showed that he *had* been scalded while taking a shower (a housemate had flushed the toilet and the water temperature shot up). This knowledge led to renewed sensitivity and caution by the young man's caregivers.

The inner voice that prevented me from teenage suicide had now assumed a different guiding role. The more I acknowledged that Asperger's Syndrome was plausible for me, the more I could fully embrace, respect, and appreciate other human beings. I became more comfortable with myself and gradually lessened my hold on the reins of control—no easy feat for someone with Asperger's and an innate need for control! My willingness to release strengthened tenfold in my work. And I began to realize that the work predicated from a spiritual connectedness. It was, quite simply, all about love.

Loving a Higher Power allowed me to become spiritual like so many others with autism, deeply appreciating the beauty in everyone and everything; delighting in the seemingly simple but vastly complex intricacies of nature; breathing in fresh air and the scent it brings; and enjoying the physical characteristics that make each human being a unique work of art. I slowly experienced a rebirth, and my sensitivity for others enhanced dramatically. For the first time in my life *people began to interest me*, and I resigned to allow God's will to unfold.

four

Spiritual Protectors

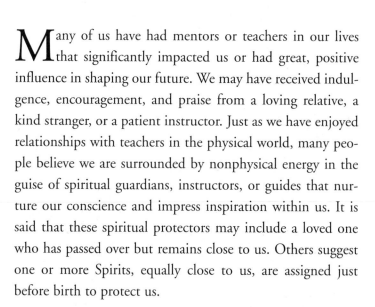

M any of us have had mentors or teachers in our lives
that significantly impacted us or had great, positive
influence in shaping our future. We may have received indul-
gence, encouragement, and praise from a loving relative, a
kind stranger, or a patient instructor. Just as we have enjoyed
relationships with teachers in the physical world, many people believe we are surrounded by nonphysical energy in the
guise of spiritual guardians, instructors, or guides that nur-
ture our conscience and impress inspiration within us. It is
said that these spiritual protectors may include a loved one
who has passed over but remains close to us. Others suggest
one or more Spirits, equally close to us, are assigned just
before birth to protect us.

Each of us inhabits a physical shell, a human body that
bears a brilliant, nonphysical energy source or soul. While
our flesh and bones are temporary and vulnerable, the soul is
invincible and inextinguishable. It is eternal and emanates
pure love. When our physical shell is no longer of use to the
soul, it is shed and the soul returns to Spirit like a magnificent butterfly liberated from its chrysalis. As is true of us all,

people with the greatest perceived differences (including our loved ones with autism) are closely guarded through the divine grace of spiritual protectors—those souls already in Spirit. These protectors often appear to be readily accessible to many individuals with autism, as will be further explained.

To avoid confusion, I wish to make the distinction between spiritual protectors and so-called "ghosts" as I understand it from my research. Ghosts are earthbound Spirits that don't realize they no longer possess a physical body—in other words, people who don't know they're dead. They don't understand that, in order to continue the journey Heavenward, they must release themselves and reunite with the Other Side. Others deliberately resist such release. Their reasons for being earthbound are entirely legitimate to them. Some simply cannot relinquish "unfinished business." It may be an extreme, willful emotion rooted in revenge or unrequited love; or it may be an association with material possessions, or territorial harbors in a physical structure or property. Still others have passed suddenly and without warning, the victims of murder or a violent accident. We've all heard stories of ghosts who linger in certain environments for years, sometimes hundreds of years. Those most notorious become the stuff of sensationalized legend. For them, time functions differently, years pass by quickly (think of it as a perpetual dreamlike state; none of us can accurately account for time in our dreams). Eventually they respond to the constant outreach of spiritual aides from Heaven, or the Other Side, who enable them to cross over. They are so self-absorbed that, until then, they are essentially "stuck." Their confused and disoriented state is more deserving of our empathy than our fear. To them, it is *we* who are the ghostly intruders in their world. Please know that ghosts are distinctly different from spiritual guardians who exist in love in the Heavenly realm.

Personally, I have always felt a strong protective presence around me as far back as I can remember. My earliest memory of this unique protection is as a toddler, playing in the water just off shore from the beach on a lake. I couldn't have been very far out in the water, but, at that age and when one is so small, everything seems huge and far away. (I have wondered if there's not something more to the common autistic attraction of being in and near water. In addition to the pressure of its overall sensory input, might the buoyancy it offers be the closest earthly approximation to the familiar fluidity of being in Spirit?) For many years my grandparents had second homes, cottages on lakes in New Jersey. On this day, they and my parents were seated on the beach in folding chairs, straw hats, and sunglasses, chatting with one another. I somehow slipped under the water and either verbally or—more likely—in my thoughts, called out for help. I was instantly supported within a bubble that encased my head, such that I could breathe without inhaling water into my lungs. It also provided the alarming position of being able to see my family but knowing that they couldn't see or hear me! Time seemed suspended, but the entire incident probably lasted seconds, and I was pulled safely from the water.

With effort, our loved ones in Spirit are purportedly capable of "shifting frequencies," like adjusting a radio dial, in order to make their presence known in our realm. The ability to shift frequencies depends upon the receptiveness of the recipient, the will of Spirit to make contact, and the mode of conductor by which the shift occurs. The conductor may be our thinking of them in loving remembrance, or for no apparent reason, usually in a relaxed state. This is why dreams are common conductors. Our subconscious mind is relaxed, susceptible, and open to infused thoughts and information that seems "acceptable" in the context of a dream. Many of us have been vividly reunited with deceased loved ones in our sleep. We've been acclimated from our earliest recollections that, in dreams, anything is plausible.

Other conductors include glass, such as reflections in windowpanes or mirrors, and water in the form of condensation, vapor, or mist. Sudden scents that we associate with loved ones may waft through the air such as tobacco, cologne, floral, or food smells. Or we may be puzzled by "coincidental" manipulations of electricity in varied forms. The latter may manifest through flickering lamps; uncanny computer emails; cell phones and pagers with messages that prove untraceable; and radios and televisions that are manipulated by an unseen hand, or play music or programming connected in memory to a loved one. Sometimes an unusual bird or insect will suddenly appear. Occasionally, a music box, toy, or novelty-type device will activate; or a book with a relevant title will "fall" from its shelf. So often these sights, sounds, smells, and symbols are linked in our memory by a strong associative element (people with autism drawn to detail are masterful at retaining information in this manner).

For example, a neighbor recently revealed her experience with such spiritual communications. Her father had been a major league baseball player with the St. Louis Cardinals. He so loved her mother but was often absent from home during their marriage. When he passed, her father was buried with a commemorative baseball ring that later turned up in the mail on her mother's birthday, addressed in a script identical to his own. Neither the postal service nor the funeral home had a viable explanation. On other anniversaries, a solitary red cardinal (his team's mascot) appeared at her mother's house, or a single gardenia—her mother's favorite—would bud and bloom outside on an otherwise dormant bush.

We've been conditioned to react with dread in response to such occurrences courtesy of Hollywood, Stephen King, and *Night Gallery* reruns—popular culture's decidedly dark and frightening spin. Too often, subtleties of spiritual communication are blithely overlooked, repressed, or discounted. Skeptics may need unequivocally direct and blatant proof. But that would detract and undermine the communication's purpose, allaying the true focus: loving affirmation that life (and consciousness) continues beyond our physical selves. It would also create extreme fear, panic, and anxiety—the very antithesis of the communication's intent. Here is a parable that illustrates the concept of spiritual communication disregarded:

> The man whispered, "God, speak to me." And a meadowlark sang. But the man did not hear. So the man yelled, "God, speak to me." And the thunder and lightning rolled across the sky. But the man did not listen. The man looked around and said, "God, let me see you." And a star shined brightly.
>
> But the man did not see. And the man shouted, "God, show me a miracle." And a life was born.

> *But the man did not notice. So, the man cried out in*
> *despair, "Touch me, God, and let me know you are here,"*
> *whereupon, God reached down and touched the man.*
> *But the man brushed the butterfly away and walked*
> *on.*

DECODING AUTISTIC HIEROGLYPHICS

Symbolic similies are as old as Aesop's fables, the lessons of Buddha, and the teachings of Christ. Curiously, being an effective consultant requires me to extrapolate the *same kinds* of symbolic information communicated by those with autism, much in the same way that Temple Grandin has made a career of using her own autism to successfully decode animal behavior. Because so many folks with autism have limited or no speech, they may demonstrate abstract communication through their actions. Or they write or type but in an influent, seemingly cryptic manner—an autistic version of hieroglyphics. My role is to apply my unconventional logic to reinterpret these communications in ways that "fit" (recall my charades analogy) in order to winnow out the crux. I try to be as accurate as possible and still make sense for everyone else, though this mastery of metaphors is an art form unto its own.

For instance, one girl was supposedly "obsessed" with people's shoes. The longer I talked with her family and professional team, the more it became apparent that she learned a lot about people, their personalities, and demeanor by the style and condition of their shoes, their gait, and walking stride. She gathered important information in this subtle, discreet manner, as befitted her nature. She was so painfully self-conscious that she spent time staring downward, at floor level, a vantage point by which observing others' shoes would be inconspicuous.

In another instance, a young man with autism who had endured many hardships and abuses referred to himself in writing as Cinderella. He likened himself to a character equally suppressed and devalued. Cinderella was intentionally segregated, excluded due to her rank and appearance.

Similarly, one young woman was passionate for all things feminine, which included adorning herself like Miss America and fairy tale princesses. My respectful speculation was that she enjoyed a certain confidence about her physical appearance, especially while in costume. She was like a princess awaiting liberation by people who "get" her so that she might fully demonstrate the depth of her whole self. Princesses are revered for their royal status, superior beauty, kind deeds, sweetness, and ability to forgive. However, classic princesses were metaphors to this teenage girl. Like the aforementioned gentleman, she, too, identified with Cinderella as well as Snow White (who was persecuted and went into hiding until her "awakening") and Sleeping Beauty (enchanted by a spell and rendered immobile, frozen in time). I'm pleased to now report that this young woman was thrilled to attend her prom and is in the early stages of planning her wedding.

I also knew a young man who did not speak and was passionate about apples—something his caregivers found annoying and purposeless. Again, through teasing out pertinent information from those who knew him best, we established the true origin of the passion. Estranged from his mother, he had been accustomed to a high-fiber diet including lots of apples during the time he had lived at home with her. Clearly, the apples were associated with his longing each time he held, smelled, and tasted them. Given that he could not speak his desires, he independently discovered a way to conjure memories of a happier time with the one person in life he truly loved. The apples were a tangible, concrete way of reminiscing, such as others reflect upon a picture album or view a home movie.

In the same way, another man with autism "played" with a toy truck. On the surface some assumed this was because he had a childlike I.Q.; however, the toy truck was the conduit by which fond memories of his deceased father (and the happy times riding in Dad's own truck) could be replayed. Model trains, train calendars, and postcards of trains were used to reward a man with autism simply because it was believed this was his lifelong "obsession." The symbolic intent was deeper, representing strong affection for a grandfather who had passed in the man's childhood. Like the fellow who held the apples, neither of these men had access to any visual imagery of their loved ones. Instead, they used objects symbolically to trigger mind-movies.

One young boy, nonverbal and believed by all to be retarded, became very animated whenever Madonna's song "Papa Don't Preach" came over the radio. He made a point of eliciting his mother's attention at this time, especially as she was feeling pressured by relatives to institutionalize him. You see, he was using the song lyric to communicate to her. To anyone else, it was just a song. But the boy's mother wisely interpreted the words as his own when Madonna sang that she had decided to keep her baby—advice this mom took to heart.

In each preceding instance, the autistic communication wasn't to be interpreted literally; it was about what the symbol *represented*. Rather it is more often like connecting the dots in order to complete the whole picture. Grasping this concept would later serve me well. (The irony is that some people with autism need to *receive* information in ways that are very concrete and literal to best understand it.) For contrast, here's one last example of comparable symbolism in autistic communication.

Brett, now nearly sixteen, lost his mother when he was eleven. During my initial meeting with the family and extended team, I learned that his mother had passed after many years of struggling with lung cancer. It is still a difficult subject for the grieving family.

Though Brett doesn't talk, he so clearly demonstrates his desire to maintain his mother's memory and keep his family focused on what's truly important to him. He does this by regularly indicating, with gestures, that he wants his loved ones to sing "Itsy-Bitsy Spider," the theme from *Barney*, and other favorite childhood songs. Not surprisingly, these are all the songs his mother used to sing to him. Re-experiencing the songs with others incites in him laughter, great joy, and lots of eye contact. Children's songs + memories of mother + loved ones = reunited family. By sharing the songs with surviving family members, he bonds those still in his physical presence with the eternal love of his mother's Spirit.

PARALLELS WITH SPIRITUAL COMMUNICATION

Likewise, it is said that our physically departed loved ones are often near us in Spirit, trying to communicate lovingly in ways that are *identically symbolic*; desiring to prove that they're very much "alive" and present—not unlike those individuals who are perceived as severely retarded or irretrievably autistic. What I've come to learn, and what others may be challenged in understanding, is that such symbolic communications are not emphatically heralded with official proclamation and blaring trumpets announcing their arrival. On the contrary, they occur so subtly—like the butterfly that was brushed away—that many don't realize their significance because *they're just there*. They happen without any fanfare at all. This lends credence to the familiar adage that our Creator works in mysterious ways. To illustrate this, Jay, from upstate New York, was humble in sharing his own background with autism and spiritual symbolism. His experience became a personal turning point:

> My daughter is autistic and now twenty-two. Being a parent of a special needs child is not easy. It is a huge life change. Most parents kind of get an "easing off" of some things when their kids hit five or so, where they don't need quite the same kind of care. Eventually the child becomes more independent, able to dress and bathe themselves. That never happened with us. Even at twenty-two, my daughter needs help in all these areas.
>
> Back in 1994 we lost a son. He was born three months premature, and he died eight months later after living his entire life in the Neonatal Intensive Care Unit. My daughter saw him only about two or three times. My daughter can't take being in closed-in spaces, nor loud sounds, nor even quick actions—all

things which are very prevalent in a NICU. We told her she was going to go in. I was terrified because other times when she's been in stressful places she has lost it, and pulled and ripped things from the wall, etc. But she went in as calmly as anything.

My son was only about twelve inches long and did not really resemble your typical baby the first time she went in. Yet she looked at him intently, smiled at him, made some very sweet sounds, and smiled at us; and when we could tell she wanted to leave, we asked her. She answered "go" and we did, very calmly. I was amazed and very moved.

After he died and was buried, my wife and I would go and visit the grave. My daughter would sit on a stone about four or five graves down and just chatter away. She was usually focused on one particular spot and it seemed as though she was talking to someone. And she was happy. If she looked at us, I'm sure there would be nothing there that would make her feel that happy. I seriously believe that somehow he and she were communicating.

People deny things they don't understand. It seems this is even worse if someone has a disability or is autistic. They don't understand things so they attack it. Some people even go so far to have clergy people do things that common sense would dictate not to, such as two parents and a minister who had their son on the steps of the altar and were—by somewhat physical means—trying to exorcise the devil who had "overtaken" their son with autism.

As for me and my own experiences, the grieving process is always a hard process. You never do get over it; you just learn to live till it is not quite so painful, but you go through a lot of hell to get there. This one day was one of those days. I was working, and I couldn't really keep my mind on it, nor could I keep from going back over the loss of my son. I'm not one to run away from things and I believe in the psychology of things; so I thought that perhaps I really needed to go to the cemetery and think and talk to him. At the gravesite, it really was not helping. I was depressed and tears were flowing. I began to walk back towards the car. There was a hedge that goes down the row, and I was walking parallel to it. Before I started very far, I saw this butterfly. It was black with a white band. It stayed with me all the way down the path, flying above the hedge. When I got to my car, got in, and was all ready to start, it landed on my windshield directly in front of my eyes. It just sat there, probably for a good five minutes. Then it picked up and flew around in a circle or two and came back and lighted again. This time it didn't stay as long. By this time I had begun to feel that this was something very unusual (and at this time I was not prone to at all think of things like this as a sign or anything else). Then it picked up and flew around a little, it circled around the front a few more times then took off going over my left shoulder and heading towards the top of the trees. I really felt that it was some kind of connection.

I knew I was falling more and more into depression. In this time when I had this breakdown, I would go walking outside around my house and, on a few of the worst days, I would see this butterfly—just like the one at the gravesite. I live close to twenty or thirty miles away from the cemetery and besides that butterfly is not common to this area. It's common to Texas! I myself had very little faith at that time and hadn't really believed in anything for about twenty years till then. I had a very strong sense of my son being there to help me deal with it. To this day, when I have very difficult times, one of these butterflies will appear and hang around until I seem to get a hold of myself again.

It was Kyle who first introduced me to what lies beneath the surface for many people with autism, including the concept of spiritual protectors. Kyle is a young boy with brilliantly glistening eyes and a purity about him that exemplifies the words "exquisitely sensitive." He also has fine, delicate features, a sensitive demeanor, with a very quiet and soft-spoken voice. Kyle is someone who selects his spoken words carefully. The second time we met, he addressed me under his breath with, "So...we meet again."

Kyle's mother, Anne, and I met in the late 1990s at one of my Pennsylvania autism workshops. Afterward, she approached me to offer her thanks and to tell me of Kyle's struggles to assimilate in school. I gave her my contact information, and we struck up a phone relationship.

Anne eventually shared that Kyle's anxieties stemmed, in

part, from "visitations" of a presence. She believed it was her father, who passed when Kyle was two years old. Two days after Anne's father died, she noticed something unusual when she sat in her dad's old recliner with Kyle on her lap. Kyle repeatedly looked into space and put out his foot. He then quickly withdrew it, giggling as if someone tickled him. Kyle later identified his grandfather—without prompting—when viewing a photograph of the gentleman taken when he was in his thirties. (I have since learned that this kind of identification of a deceased grandparent—even if grandparent and grandchild never physically met—is a very common occurrence among people with autism of all ages.)

As Kyle grew, he would sometimes verbally express his fears in symbolic or cryptic ways, like saying, "No more twister, Mommy." My interpretation was that the "twister" might be a spiraling portal or tunnel through which her father appeared to Kyle. I advised Anne and her husband Rich to openly address Spirit, explain that his unexpected visitations were frightening to Kyle, and respectfully request that he desist.

Although Kyle seemed to be the center of the attention, his older brother also saw the presence in the family home. He described it as an older man, shuffling hunched over. Fortunately Anne and Rich validated what the boy saw. They diffused any anxieties by calmly asking him to describe what he saw, explaining that it was "okay."

During a conversation in which Anne's father was mentioned, both Anne and Rich witnessed the dining room lights flicker. Anne said out loud, "Dad, if that's you, do it again," and the lights flickered again—an example of symbolic communication from Spirit.

Anne and Rich took my advice and addressed Anne's father, and the activity temporarily stopped. But eventually unusual circumstances prevailed. Kyle often took to sleeping with his parents, or Anne would sleep with him in his bed. Once, a misplaced winter cap, given to Kyle by his grandfather, reappeared at the foot of Kyle's bed right after Anne dreamt about it materializing.

But it seemed as though Kyle was reacting to more than just his grandfather, who was surely a benign, loving presence; other influences were involved. The family asked if I would come and walk through their home to see if I sensed anything, which I did. I walked every inch of the house and gained two distinct impressions. The first was that Anne and Rich's bedroom had a "heavy," oppressive atmosphere to it. This lightened throughout the rest of the house but was densest there. The family's newly built kitchen addition felt "buoyant" and light, the opposite of the master bedroom. The family confirmed that Kyle shared my identical impressions.

On this visit, the family had some photographs from a recent outing. Kyle was always attracted to soldiers and horses, and enjoyed trips to the Gettysburg battlefield. The photographs were varied groupings of family members taken in select areas or in front of certain monuments. Kyle appeared relaxed and at ease in some of the group shots. In others, though, he had a tense expression on his face and his little fists were clenched. In these same photographs, streaks of light are present in the sky around Kyle. These streaks are not present in any photographs other than those in which Kyle seems distressed.

Another hurdle for Kyle was his relationship with Rich's

father, who lived on a nearby farm. On many occasions, Kyle became completely petrified while visiting the farm. His anxiety grew to the point of becoming physically ill and throwing up if the subject of visiting the farm was even discussed. The intervention here needed to be twofold.

First, Rich's father needed support in understanding that this was not a reaction to him personally, even though Kyle shied from him when he came to the family's home. Understandably, Kyle associated this grandfather with whatever unpleasantness transpired at the farm. Once the family made clear that he was no longer expected to visit the farm, Kyle's relationship with his grandfather gradually softened.

Second, I requested that the family investigate the farm's history. Who lived there prior to Rich's father, and what exactly happened to the former owners? What the family discovered was that several members of the former owner's family died in or around the farm area; a couple of the deaths were accidental. What seemed obvious was that Kyle perceived legitimate "ghosts" when visiting the farm, which terrorized him.

The family eventually moved to a new house. I aided them in supporting Kyle to prepare for the move, giving him a sense of ownership in the new place. At last report, the most antagonistic presences seem to have followed the family, but the activity has lessened in intensity. It is no longer the derailing distraction it had once been for Kyle.

Supporting Kyle and his family in the context of an educational team was a delicate process. Respecting the family's wise wishes, we never broached the subject of Kyle's gifts of perception. As I've observed, the caveat that lies in wait around every corner is one of misinterpretation and accusation of "psychotic" or "delusional behavior." Instead I elicited from the team their definitions of the words "exquisitely sensitive." Without saying anything more, we laid a foundation within which we could communicate comfortably and freely.

My wish for Kyle is that his family will continue supporting him to understand his unique gift. Our mutual wish is that someday Kyle will know how best to employ his gift to the good and great benefit of others.

FRANK CHECKS IN

Similar to Kyle's parents, Anne and Rich, I, too, determined to address the presence that existed in my life, saving me in the eleventh hour and guiding my intuitions. That this guardian originated in a Higher Power was certain to me. But all my life this unseen protector had been anonymous. So I did the next best thing and christened it with a name of my own in order to create familiarity and personalize the relationship. "Frank" was the name I pulled from nowhere in particular. Within a week, I received a strong validation. I was enmeshed in housework, having been away on business all week when the doorbell rang. It was a young man in his twenties. He was driving the garbage truck that day and had accidentally backed into my mailbox post. He wanted to know if I would come and take a look. From where I stood, it looked fine but upon close inspection, the pine of the main post, while still intact, had been split vertically down the center. I asked if the waste management service had liability for this sort of thing. He went back into his truck to scribble down some information.

When he handed me the slip of paper, I saw that it was his personal name, number, and address. I wondered if the company wouldn't simply cover the cost, and the young man explained it would. But then I asked, "If I report this to them, does that put you in any jeopardy?" He said it would reflect negatively on his driving record. He had given me his personal information with the hope of paying for a replacement himself. I took the information for both contacts, and told him I'd make a decision and get back to him. I also let him know how much I appreciated his honesty.

A couple hours later, I determined to give him the benefit of the doubt and allow him to obtain a replacement post as he had offered. I found his slip of paper and looked again at the notes he had written. There, in his own hand, was his contact information. His name was Frank. Once again, I had been oblivious to the obvious in the moment. I saw his name when he handed the paper to me originally but at the time nothing registered. Not only was his name Frank, it soon dawned on me that the definition of Frank's last name, Ward, pertains to the act of keeping guard, or guardianship. In essence, his name translates to "Frank the Guardian." It couldn't have been more succinct.

Now that I knew the young man was a "Frank," I was even gentler with him on the phone, and let him know again how much I valued his honesty. What Frank Ward told me weeks later—which I hadn't known at the time—was that he wasn't even supposed to have been there that day. It was his first time in the area because he was filling in for someone else. His regular driving route was many miles away. Understand that Frank Ward, himself, was not necessarily a messenger or even someone I could trust to keep his word (he eventually did). It's what he *symbolized* that was the intended communication.

A PROTECTIVE PRESENCE

Mark Sachnik is a self-advocate with autism and vice president of the Autism Society of Collin County in Dallas, Texas. Now in his late forties, Mark reflected on a similar spiritual presence in his life that always provided protection from real harm.

> I walked away from many extremely dangerous situations and near-death experiences virtually unscathed. There is absolutely no way I should have come away from taking a direct hit from a car going thirty miles an hour with nothing more than a double compound fracture on my right leg. It just so happened that the accident occurred no more than one hundred yards away from a fire/police station.
>
> There are numerous other examples of walking away from accidents and situations I attribute to divine intervention. Examples include walking away from several high-speed bicycle crashes and one high-speed motorcycle wipe out in the middle of a freeway with nothing more than bumps and bruises; riding my bicycle to work for four years to a job location in the most crime-ridden part of New Orleans and no one ever even laid a hand on me; and running full speed into the deep end of a swimming pool (I was five years old and definitely displaying "autistic"

symptoms) at the same time my father just happened to walk out of the motel room to get something from the car. Somehow I managed to wander around one of the most dangerous areas in Corpus Christi (at a time when I displayed significant "autistic" symptoms) without so much as a scratch or worse. I got through numerous potentially serious "mugging" and "bullying" incidents in school without sustaining any real serious damage.

A loving and protective presence also surrounds Patrick (from our last chapter). Doreen, Patrick's mom, told me that one day, while nursing her youngest child, she found herself distraught with worry about Patrick's future. Just then, she felt a hand on her head and heard a voice telling her Patrick would be fine. She said that ever since, Patrick has defied real physical harm. Doreen has observed him walk across broken glass on the kitchen floor without being cut and hold a shattered light fixture that was still plugged in, evading electrocution. She's watched as Patrick routinely teeters and dances around the perimeter lip of the family's above ground swimming pool without losing balance and falling. Doreen also saw Patrick sitting at rapt attention on a stool while alone in the family barn, apparently interacting with someone visible only to him.

THE GRANDPARENT BOND

Christine is a mom from California who initially contacted me when she learned I was broaching the subject of spirituality in people with autism. In an exhilarating turn of events, she followed up several weeks later to share an amazing footnote to her story, as you'll read. Christine's first communication was September 26, 2002. She wrote:

> My son, Justin, is six years old and has been diagnosed with autism for three years. He is high-functioning and verbal. He speaks most words and phrases literally because he has a difficult time with abstract thinking. Last July my sister, Justin, and I were driving in the car when out of the blue, he said (off topic), "Mamma (my mom) is going to die in eighty-eight days." I asked him how he knew that, and he said he just *knew*.
>
> Eighty-eight days will be this Sunday. Last week my mom had a massive stroke. Right now she is on hospice with comfort measures, and they do not expect her to live longer than the end of this week. She is in a comatose state.
>
> I am not shocked that Justin predicted this. My mom has had stroke-related dementia since before Justin was born, but they have always had this very close, nonverbal relationship. He can "read" her in ways other people cannot.

Christine graciously added the following postscript to Justin's story a couple weeks later:

> My mom died two hours after I sent you the original post on September 26. She didn't make it the eighty-eight days like Justin predicted, but was three days

shy. Justin woke up about 3:00 a.m. and was crying. He said he had a scary dream. About five minutes later, my sister called and said we needed to get [to the nursing home], that mom was not doing well. Then she called right back and said that she had died.

Justin does not have scary dreams. Honestly, I cannot remember a time he has ever said he had a bad dream or has woken up from it. Dreams are not concrete or literal. But there were so many other weird "messages" that happened during all of this as well.

My sister left the nursing home on September 25, 2002, at 7:40 p.m. I know this was the exact time because she called me on her cell phone as she was walking out, and my phone has caller ID with the date and time someone calls. When we went down to the nursing home after mom had died, I casually glanced at the clock; the second hand was still moving, but the clock had stopped at 7:42 p.m. Was it my mom acknowledging that my sister was there and everything was okay?

Justin is very intuitive and picks up on emotion but doesn't know what to do with it. He has said several times over the last two weeks that Mamma is here and not to be sad. He makes these abstract statements in present tense, such as, "Mamma says she loves you," and was in his bedroom the other day humming a tune that my mom used to sing to me when I was little and to my oldest son when he was a baby. She did not sing this to Justin because by the time he was born her Alzheimer's was so advanced, she couldn't remember the song.

I guess what I find so unusual about this is that Justin is very literal. That is just how he speaks. He talks exactly how he sees things and has very concrete thinking.

Christine and Justin's story so beautifully illustrates several themes. The first is the *very strong* connection that many people with autism feel for their grandparents. The bond may be so strong that it sometimes supersedes immediate family relations. The second theme is that love is all-powerful and transcends physical boundaries. The love Christine's mother gave her family—and Justin in particular—is seamless despite her transition from the physical realm to the spiritual one. Finally, there are the validations that Christine has received. If she was ever in doubt, she should be no longer. Justin, in his purity and innocence, is clearly a conduit between his grandmother and his family. His grandmother's deteriorated physical state, while in the final stages of Alzheimer's here on earth, was of no consequence when it came to contacting Justin. She lulled him with a song he wouldn't otherwise have known, or infused him with communications so that he is now a messenger to the family. And the message is that his grandmother is here with everyone and loving them all more than ever before.

Wouldn't it be fascinating to know if Justin's grandmother had been reciprocating communication with him *through* the physical "shell" of Alzheimer's in the same way that Christine maintained that Justin could "read" her? Many believe that even when the physical body is ill or disabled, spiritual power is never diminished. Author Sylvia Browne proposes, "If you have a loved one suffering from...Alzheimer's disease...never doubt that their wide awake, eternal Spirits hear and thrive in all the joyful affirmations you can offer."

Similar to Kyle's experiences, Justin's initial "scary" dream may have been another premonition like the one that he had originally, which concerned a painful, unexpected physical loss of someone dear to him. Justin's story is a glorious example of eternal love everlasting.

Another loving validation of a spiritual protector supporting someone with autism comes from Maria, of Virginia. Maria lost her father in 2002 but has been comforted in knowing that his presence is near to Jack, her six-year-old son.

> I have asked Jack if his grandfather comes to see him in his dreams or in quiet times, and he says yes but cannot or will not elaborate. I know in my heart that he is near him all the time. It may sound silly, but on my birthday this year my son, who could never ride his tricycle, began peddling all around our neighborhood. I had wished for that for so long, and my father knew this. I know in my heart it was a birthday gift from him.

Ursula's son Singen seems to also enjoy the protection of a grandparent in Spirit. Ursula told me of Singen's close call with drowning when he was about two years old during which he appeared to have been intercepted mid-fall.

> Once he had gotten out of our house, and I didn't realize it. We had a big pool off the patio, and it was

fenced in but not from one door. I heard a sound knocking on the door and when I went to answer it, there stood Singen, soaking wet from the waist up…and totally dry from the waist down. It looked as if someone took him by the ankles and dipped him in the pool headfirst but stopped at his waist (a definite line of wet to dry). I was shocked and thankful for whatever or whoever was his savior that day. I also had help in raising him in his younger times. Whenever he would be getting into some kind of trouble and I was in a different part of the house a woman would call me. From the smell of her rose perfume, I always felt it was his Grandma Kit.

Sherry and her family live in western Pennsylvania where she is mother to three beautiful little boys. Her oldest child, Buck, who is eight years old, experiences autism. Since spending time with his team I've seen him begin to blossom, and he is talking more than ever. I've told Sherry that Buck is so physically exquisite, his face is literally like that of an angel: flawless porcelain skin, gentle blue eyes full of inner wisdom, achingly perfect features, and a halo of blond hair. During a break in my first consultation with Buck's team, I felt compelled to ask Sherry privately, "Does he 'read' you?" She knew exactly what I meant, and with glistening eyes, replied simply, "Yes." To be in Buck's presence is a glorious privilege, and I cherish the drawings he's made for me.

Sherry wrote:

My mom was the most excited person to know that I was having a baby. Sadly, she died two weeks after Buck was born. She had only gotten to see him a couple of times.

When Buck was about seven months old, at bedtime, I would put him in his crib upstairs in our house with the monitor on downstairs so that I could hear him. At least two nights a week, Buck would begin laughing (not a little giggle, really laughing!) as if someone was tickling him. When I would go up to check on him, he would be looking in one spot as if he was seeing something or someone. At first it gave me an eerie feeling, but then I would think maybe he was seeing my mom.

Buck was four when Luke [Sherry's youngest child] was born and was still not verbal. But, as soon as Luke was old enough to talk, he started telling me things about him and Buck. He would refer to him and Buck "when they were big." He would tell me that they lived in a castle and that they fought in the army together. Also, anytime we would mention Heaven, Luke's eyes would light up and he would say how beautiful it was, and go on to tell about the castle that he and Buck lived in.

Luke then started telling me that he knew his "other" grandma. He said he was with her when she died in the hospital (nobody had ever told him that she was in a hospital when she died). He would also tell me stories about her being in our house and playing with him. I would wonder if he was telling me things that

Buck knew but couldn't talk enough to tell me about.

Then I was talking to a woman in our area that seems to "know" things. She told me that my mother came back to help Buck and that he sees her a lot but cannot tell me. She also told me that Luke knows this and that he would tell me about it!

Now that Buck is talking more, he has told me some things before they happened. Small things such as a hotel room number we would be staying in before we got there, what's for lunch in school before the menu comes out, and dates that we would be doing things before we knew them. He has told me things that he remembers when he was just a baby. I have one picture of my mom holding him when he was a week old. If I show it to him, he says he remembers it and knows it's his grandma.

Buck recently found a small picture of Jesus that had been put away. He got so excited when he saw this. He said, "I remember Jesus in our old house [meaning the family's former home]. He touched me right here," and pointed to his shoulder.

Now that he is talking this much, I am so excited to hear more about what he knows.

Once again, Sherry's offerings validate that the love expressed by her sons' grandmother is so powerful that it is unaffected by earthly bonds. Note, too, that Buck is jubilant upon discovering a long lost image of Christ, whom he recalls fondly.

Sherry's story also speaks to two of her sons having previously known each other as soldiers in another time. They are joined in partnership again in the present. In his book, *Coming Back*, Dr. Raymond Moody speaks to the banality of many past lives in his research: "Most aren't royalty or members of the elite. For the most part, they are slaves or gladiators, soldiers, or stable boys." Another friend with autism indicated, "I think I was a doctor of medicine." This made sense because he has long held the desire to write a book on eating disorders despite being without any clinical knowledge. However, in other instances, adults and children with autism have revealed that they led previous lives as persons of high religious standing. One young man was ardent in expressing his sense of dichotomy in consciousness, what he described as being a "holy man," when he communicated, "I am one man in one skin and another man in Christ."

Like Shawn, Reneé of Opelousas, Louisiana, told me of her six-year-old son's spiritual capacity.

> I have a son named Gabriel who is autistic and truly a messenger from Heaven…He has been categorized as mildly mentally retarded yet the school evaluation does not conclusively label him autistic…I always felt Gabriel would be my messenger from Heaven. Even when I was pregnant I knew my son would be special. Well, now that the severity of his condition is becoming more evident; at six years old it just keeps getting more difficult. But the good news is I will not give up on him or my advocacy efforts.
>
> Since age two, Gabriel has had a few demonstrations that he has some spiritual capabilities. One event was at the death of his grandfather. After the

funeral, we went home and he fell asleep next to me as I stayed up to write. Later, he sat up in bed and said, "Pa Ben," and pointed towards the foot of the bed. He smiled and lay back down and went back to sleep. I cried because I know that Gabriel saw his grandpa that evening.

Several times since then, Gabriel has pointed and said "Charlene." We used to live in a community that investigated the merits of a young girl, Charlene, who died of leukemia. Some claim she is a saint. Gabriel's pa died of leukemia and prayed with references to this young girl. Now, the question of Catholic beliefs might influence one to disregard this testimony. Regardless, I know Gabriel has some special gift that will eventually become more evident.

I have a picture of Gabriel lying down. When I got the picture back, a cloudy mist was over his head. I never knew how to interpret this, other than it was a sign that he is special.

NATIVE AMERICAN CONNECTIONS

Curiously enough, in addition to grandparents, Native Americans are often perceived as Spirit protectors. This is true of Matt, a midstate Pennsylvania high school senior with Asperger's Syndrome. Matt revealed a childhood experience:

When I was young around two or three years old, a Spirit visited me. The Spirit was of a well-known Native American named Samoset. We talked a lot during the nighttime and I learned a few things about

Native Americans from him. Today I am age eighteen and have not heard from Samoset in a long time. But what I discovered is that I was really sensitive to Spirit's presence at a young age. Today, I have had other encounters but haven't really been able to talk to any other Spirits since my childhood years.

Susan contacted me from her home in Norfolk, Virginia, after several other moms had seen me make a presentation in the area. She told me of the loving bond that perseveres between her spouse and daughter, colored by their rich Native American heritage.

William "Billy" Seeking Golden Eagle of the Rainbow is the father of my twice-exceptional daughter Emilie. He was a Native American of the Cherokee Indians. He died a tragic death resulting from a gunshot wound to the heart. He was high-functioning autistic, as his daughter is. I believe he had—and has—the ability to communicate with Spirits and from the Spirit side of what we know, even with our lack of scientifically measuring this unusual phenomenon.

Two weeks after his death, I found his birth certificate lying on the floor in the pathway of my kitchen and living room. It had some how slipped out from my daughter's baby book on the second shelf of a bookcase by the door. I picked it up and said "What am I not seeing here I have not seen before?" Billy applied for the reissue of the certificate when looking for work in 1991. On the birth certificate was the date issued April 18, 1991. My daughter Em was born a year later to the day, April 18, 1992. I clearly heard Billy say, "If Em ever doubts how connected she is to me show her this certificate." My daughter was one-and-a-half years of age at this time.

I also was guided to look on the back of a picture of Billy holding Em. Unbeknownst to me he had written "Em, I love you more than I know how to. Love, DaDa." This is the same remarkable daughter who came into a Native American Ceremonial site at age six and walked up to the tree that many ceremonial dancers had prayed upon for a three-day dance and fast. When placing her hand at the spot where I had prayed, it was like an electrical current shocked her. Em pulled her hand back quickly. I said "What did you feel Em?" She said "My dad." Em says when she feels her father's presence, she experiences a tingly feeling in her body all over. Her connection and relationship with her father's Spirit delves deep in the Native American roots, much of which would take the understanding of an individual who follows the Native American belief system.

Recently, at age thirteen, she has been questioning why she is so connected and drawn to the number thirteen. She drew a license plate "WHY 13." Well, I said, your father's Spirit staff he made that hangs over your bed has thirteen eagle feathers hanging on it; his birthday was on the thirteenth; and your medicine name that was gifted to you in ceremony at age seven is Turtle Woman Nation. There are thirteen moons on the turtle's back (on every turtle shell there are thirteen sections).

Em's personal totems are the Raven and Crow. So when she is in need of support, I believe her father sends omens of these birds as a way to show that he is with her. Yesterday morning, during her three-day suspension from school for crawling under a desk and not coming out, we had a young crow learning to fly come in our yard. Em got to see the parent trying to show the young crow how to fly.

In *The Mystic Heart*, Brother Wayne Teasdale's excellent and comprehensive study of comparable mystic themes intertwined throughout the world's spiritual traditions, the concept of animal spirit guides is discussed. Teasdale writes, "Native Americans know that all beings are part of the web of life, and we have responsibilities to this great web of interconnection. Native cultures are keenly aware that nature, earth, the Great Spirit, and the spirit guides have taught them everything they know." Teasdale states that encounters with an animal guide or totem, such as Em's crow, are "common in the experience of Indians and other indigenous peoples, and their sacred literatures are filled with such examples." The animal totem-as-spiritual-message-bearer theme also figures into the following parable from Canadian autism consultant Gail Gillingham.

I am working with a five year old whose father has some North American Native blood. This winter a rabbit appeared in their front yard and it would sit, calmly staring in the window at them for hours. This in the middle of a city with a population of over a million people. The father finally decided that the rabbit may be some kind of a spirit guide and so he asked his daughter one day, as the rabbit sat there, what she thought the rabbit was trying to tell them. Her immediate response was, "Be calm about autism." Once the daughter shared this message with her father, the rabbit left and has not returned.

Many of us recognize that we *all* have a spiritual presence about us—this experience is not exclusive to people with autism. Some of us may have parents, grandparents, or children that have passed on with whom we still talk to. While love is eternal, some of us have regrets for not having expressed our love for others while they are still present with us—this lesson is most important of all.

A Spiritual Awakening

I found myself pondering so many aspects of my life as a result of those early meetings with Kyle and his family. As I came to embrace my personal spirituality, my emergence steadily progressed. But there remained a yearning unfulfilled: Could I rediscover the little boy who once sobbed for Christ with all his heart in a church pew so long ago? This awaited future resolution; however, during this reawakening, a powerful dream experience occurred. In it, the post-traumatic stress that I experienced from having been verbally and physically abused by peers as a child (which haunted me into adulthood) resolved completely.

In the dream, all of my known adversaries were seated at a large, long table, like a dining room table with lots of extra leaves. While they were seated, I was—interestingly enough and symbolically—*standing*. I walked behind them and, one by one, leaned down to kiss each on the cheek in an act of forgiveness. Thereafter I was healed and never again plagued by the nightmares of abuse.

By the spring of 2000, a small group of three professional acquaintances began meeting to explore holistic possibilities related to supporting people with autism and others. I asked if I could join their discussions; their camaraderie and like thinking felt great. I was feeling rejuvenated but increasingly pulled to do something more. I gained confidence toward making the rather momentous decision with which I was faced: leaving my nine-to-five job in order to become self-employed as an autism consultant was inevitable. Still, self-doubt and financial security swayed me from taking the plunge.

I had never before directly asked God for anything because I always thought it selfish. I figured that people in far worse situations than I truly deserved His time and attention. But in this instance, I didn't feel I had any other option. I desperately needed help and guidance in making a pivotal decision. While at home one day I asked God for just that. I requested that the answer be revealed to me in a dream. I promptly lay down to take a nap and…nothing happened. I had a very standard, run-of-the-mill dream that held no special significance for me. How audacious of me to presume that God would tend to my needs on demand, I thought! However, that very night—when I no longer expected it—I experienced a dream so powerful and vivid that its message was clearer to me than anything I'd ever felt.

In the dream, I observed a young boy, a student with autism, in an unfamiliar classroom setting. I sensed that the student wasn't intended to be a specific person; he represented anyone for whom I could provide support, guidance, and encouragement. The boy was unable speak but was, instead, interacting with his teacher by touching a computer screen.

Seeing me, the boy turned to face me, and I lovingly told him how very proud I was of him. He then showed me a book, which he opened in the middle to display a large, three-dimensional paper pop-up of a white, winged horse. He placed the book on the floor, and the horse grew to actual size, large enough for the boy to mount. Once astride the horse, he was levitated upwards and off the ground. I watched as he soared up above the treetops and house roofs until he slowly and gently came back to earth, like a falling leaf. I asked him, "How did that feel?" He looked at me, grinned broadly, and beamed radiantly. Then he smiled and *spoke*, "It felt great!"

In that exact moment, I awakened shortly after 1:00 a.m. with a tingling, electrical sensation surging down the length of my body. This was paired with an immediate understanding. If I interpreted the dream literally, the sky was the limit where my calling and its possibilities were concerned. I knew then that my prayer, my request of God, had been so beautifully answered. I could give notice at work, forfeiting my salary and benefits—with nothing else to go to—knowing that I would be just fine. And I have been ever since.

In meeting with my colleagues shortly thereafter, I related my dream. Two of them practically yelped, instantly recognizing its significance. They maintained that, according to Native American beliefs, *I* was the white horse in the dream that had enabled the boy to grow and soar. Accordingly, they read aloud, "Horse enables shamans to fly through the air and reach Heaven...Before Horse, humans were earthbound, heavy-laden and slow [the same disparaging description has certainly been applied to persons with autism]. Once humans climbed on Horse's back, they were as free and fleet as the wind."

A specific description of the white horse, and all it represents, lent further credence to the dream. The description read, in part, "White stallion was the message carrier for all the other horses, and represented wisdom in power." The narrative went on to discuss the white horse's conversation with Dreamwalker, a shaman on a journey to heal another in need. The horse continued (with my italics added for emphasis), "You have the knowledge through humility that you are an instrument of Great Spirit. *As I carry you upon my back*, you carry the needs of the people on yours. In wisdom, you understand that power is not given lightly but awarded to those who are willing to carry responsibility in a balanced manner."

I soon discovered that horses are ancient archetypes of strength and classic symbols of having accomplished a new level of earthly wisdom. Additional research revealed that Dionysius the Areopagite wrote, "The shining white horses denote clear truth and that which is perfectly assimilated to the divine light." And the Book of Revelation references Christ's second coming astride a white horse, denoting purity and faithfulness. Given its history of powerful symbolism in a range of spiritual beliefs, I could have asked for no clearer sign than that of the white horse. I was now willing to accept the responsibility.

five

Angels in the Atmosphere

Angels are present in every religion of every culture worldwide. They are referenced in mythology, folklore, and Scripture passages in the Bible. Angels are messengers of divine proportions, bearing communications originating in the Creator's perfection. Historically, their other functions have been to inspire, guide, and protect human beings. Angels are not only all-knowing, but also magnificently all-loving.

Angels are stunning to behold. Their exquisite beauty renders them indescribable. Sanjay, a poet with autism, confirmed, "When we speak about angels, our words are inadequate." In traditional religious depiction, angels appear to mortals in all their winged and haloed and glowing glory. It is not unrealistic that such an ancient entity should appear in this manner, in modern times, to our jaded eyes. Sanjay added, "The question is not if they exist but how we recognize their presence in our lives." Many believe angels are able to assume whatever appearance is most palatable for us to receive them, without being conspicuous if they so choose. Will, a brilliant young adult with autism, agreed, "Angels do not come in white robes and wings but in the guise of people we have loved. The angels know we will welcome them if they look like people we can love."

Angels have never been human, but, on occasion, they can take human *form*. There are many recent books filled with anecdotes of angels intervening and aiding others in both direct and subtle ways. In *Pretending to be Normal*, Dr. Liane Holliday Willey, a person self-identified with Asperger's Syndrome, relates an experience with such a savior in a time of crisis, even though in her book she does not ascribe any spiritual allusions to the incident.

Liane accompanied her husband on a business trip and became terribly disoriented when venturing out alone into San Francisco. She soon found herself lost in an unsafe part of town, being converged upon by a crowd of homeless people. In her moment of greatest duress, a well-dressed and very large stranger driving an expensive car appeared next to her. His mere presence provided her protection from harm and enabled her to calm and focus. The man seemed to know how to redirect her back to her hotel in the very clear, concrete manner that she would best understand. He then stood by as she returned to her car and drove off. Liane also mentions how she still sees him in dreams in which she replays the incident.

In another instance, Liane was rescued from an uncertain encounter with an intruder in her university classroom early one morning. At a critical moment, a student just happened into the room and intervened any potential altercation.

Over dinner with Patrick and his family (whom I've mentioned previously), I discussed development of this book project and gave examples of the divine experiences of others, including contact with angels. At this, Patrick's eyes lit up and he became quite elated. Seemingly filled with unspoken knowledge, he bounced up and down in his chair with joy.

On another evening, fourteen-year-old Kevin reacted similarly when I had the same conversation with him. His five-year-old niece nonchalantly explained that she and "Uncle Kevin" (whom she adores) often talk without using spoken words. She added that an angel told her Kevin was here to teach a special lesson. And indeed, we are clearly Kevin's pupils. He is intensely passionate about the exquisite, classical compositions of Mozart, Beethoven, and Bach, and, while he rarely speaks, he will hum or "sing" to the music.

When I came to see Kevin, he was outside, barefoot in the dirt driveway, awaiting my arrival. In synchronicity, Kevin and I walked toward each other and, simultaneously in that moment, we each raised a hand to lovingly cup the side of one another's face such that we looked like a mirror image. It was amazing.

During our first break in the consultation, I stood to stretch and admiringly surveyed the Spartan kitchen and its simple, homey decor. Among the knick-knacks on a shelf near the sink was an inconspicuous figurine—an angel. As I lifted the angel from her spot, Kevin *audibly spoke*, "Amen." It was not unlike the cathartic dream I had had with the white, winged horse and the silent boy who uttered adoringly to me.

Soon after that evening, Kevin's mother, Eileen, wrote with a validation. Hers was a beautiful, perfect example of "making miracles" in motion, stemming from renewed respect for Kevin.

I just wanted to let you know about two break-throughs with my dude. On Sunday, I asked the kids what they wanted for lunch. To my surprise, this time Kevin not only got what he wanted out of the fridge, but he *told* [our family] that he wanted hot dogs and milk! He actually *said it*. I thought I was hearing things until Justin yelped, "Did you hear that? He talked!" Then this morning, he imitated Jesse. I scolded him for something and he said, "My bad," and "Gonna kick the butt!"

Several months later, Eileen added that Kevin was steadily improving. He was even talking to his teacher and speech therapist now. He'd tell his teacher "No, don't want to," when he wasn't in the mood to do something. He was also answering yes and no questions with much more accuracy. These were profound, unprecedented achievements for Kevin.

Mark Sachnik from Texas summarized his beliefs about angels and autism:

There are many times I have taken time to sit back and wonder why some things in my life have unfolded the way they have (both good and bad). After careful examination, I began to realize that the fact that I am here doing this email is in itself an act of God and a very good guardian angel.

One form of spirituality is an event or series of events that because of timing or simply that it is so out of the ordinary…cannot be explained with logic. Many would attribute those events as a result of "dumb" luck, while those with strong religious beliefs will attribute these events to God's intervention or having a "guardian angel" watching over us. I think the fact that there are folks like you, Jerry Newport, Stephen Shore, Temple Grandin, and myself who face the challenges of being adults with autism but are still able to progress to the point where we can compete successfully in the academic and business world and come to terms with our challenges to the point where we are able and willing to share our experiences with the community is definitely a manifestation of God's works.

As part of the second day of a two-day autism workshop, I ask that participants form small workgroups to analyze and deconstruct several different scenarios based upon real people. The final anecdote concerns a young boy struggling in school. The last sentence concerns the boy's reports that he "sees things."

Often, groups processing the remainder of the scenario overlook this detail, and I must draw their attention to it. Some people respond creatively by rightly speculating that, like many others with autism, the boy is visually replaying something in his mind. Others offer adjunct theories; one is that he may be hallucinating. After this discussion, I ask them to now reconsider the situation in terms of the phrase "exquisitely sensitive." This is when people will usually begin to define the phrase "exquisitely sensitive" as the ability to perceive things that most others cannot.

Recently, a group I facilitated was still stuck about how to respond. I encouraged them to take whatever they were thinking to a higher level. One gentleman who had not spoken for the entire two days thus far, softly said, "Spiritual." What a wonderful opportunity to validate his participation and brilliant thinking! It was then, while the room was silent from everyone absorbing so much information over the past two days that I ventured into uncharted territory. I invited them to consider it not uncommon for people with autism to possess exquisite sensitivities, and listed several examples, like those in this book.

At this point in the workshop, people are usually moved, awed, or dumbstruck by unconsidered possibilities. On one occasion, a young woman who was visibly upset approached me afterward with a tearful confession. She had once been responsible for recommending that a woman with autism be prescribed strong antipsychotic medications. Why? Because the woman with autism told this person that she saw angels around her.

Donelle is a parent from California who wrote me about Tanya, her eight-year-old daughter with high-functioning autism. Her first sentence surely got my attention. Donelle wrote pointedly: "My...daughter sees angels, God, and Heaven—and I believe she does—although I don't know whether it is in her imagination or what." My advice to Donelle and other caregivers is that it is healthy to be skeptical, but please don't overlook the obvious—a lesson I've had to learn time and again. Many of you who love and care for someone with autism already know that often such folks are extremely literal and concrete in their interpretation of everyone and everything about them. Accept at face value that to which you are privileged to bear witness as it unfolds before you. As we'll see, Tanya's experiences are consistent with those of others with an autistic way of being.

Donelle continued:

> I can tell you, as an outsider looking in, that I have watched Tanya pray and have instantly seen a response. It is amazing to me. I can also show you pictures she has drawn. In one particular picture that I love, she drew the Nativity but not from the perspective that one normally sees. Her picture is drawn as if she was floating above the scene, or an angel's view. There have been other times when she points to the sky and tells me that she can see Heaven. She'll point right to it and tell me it is right there.

My friend Debbie told me that she now understood there was no cause for alarm when she observed Scott, her teenage son with autism and Down Syndrome, talking and smiling while "alone" in his room. She wrote:

> My first experience with what I now know to be angels was three weeks before Scott was born. I was at Giant Eagle [a supermarket] and a man with Down Syndrome named John was there. He lived in a group home. I saw him at Giant Eagle usually once a week and he would always approach me to talk. On this particular day John touched my very pregnant belly and the baby lurched. John smiled broadly and commented to me "Your baby is just like me!" I

was confused and said "John, what do you mean? I am going to have a boy?" and he commented again "Your baby is just like me!" I didn't think too much more about it until I went into labor three weeks later and delivered Scott. When the doctor told me that Scott had Down Syndrome, a calm came over me, and I realized John was giving me information that I would need to accept the precious gift that was given to me.

When Scott was about a month old, I had a talk with Diane, a dear friend who is a Mormon. I told her about my experience with John, and she patted my hand and said, "Debbie I wanted to share a thought with you, but I thought you might think I was a bit crazy. After hearing about your encounter with John I think you might understand what I am going to tell you." Diane then proceeded to tell me that Mormons believe in reincarnation. I remember rolling my eyes and thinking "Yes, Diane is just a tad wacky!" She laughed at my reaction and continued with her thoughts. She told me that she personally believed that people with Down Syndrome were "angels" that had reached the highest level but loved being with the human race so much that they came back to teach us the ultimate lesson. That lesson was absolute acceptance and love. At the time I thought it was a very nice sentiment but, again, my heart did not fully understand.

Scott was always a very happy baby. He would coo and laugh and would appear at times to be carrying on a conversation with someone that only he could see. Many times he would be up at odd hours or most of the night, but the next morning he wouldn't appear to be tired or out of sorts.

This pattern has continued through to today. He is nineteen years old now. Scott has a dual diagnosis of Down Syndrome and autism. He is considered nonverbal, but he can talk and chooses when and who to talk to. There are many times that I am awakened at night to hear him giggling and laughing and talking in a language that I do not understand. Then I will hear him saying, "Shhhhh, she'll hear. Shhhhh." When I knock and enter his room he is very welcoming and will say, "It's alright, Ma's here" and he will laugh. When I ask, "Scott, who are you talking to?" He answers, "It's the angels, Ma."

I will ask him, "Scott, are you really an angel?" and he smiles and does his sign that indicates that what I have asked him is correct. Then he hugs and kisses me and tells me I am sweet. He also looks directly into my and his father's eyes. The look is so intense that you can actually feel it touching your soul.

My husband and I were able to take a trip to Mexico two years ago. On the day that we left for home we were at the airport waiting for the plane to come home. I was bored so I walked around the airport looking into the shop windows. As I was walking back to where my husband was seated, a man ran towards me and stopped in my path. He reached out and touched my face and looked into my eyes in the same manner that Scott does. The man had Down Syndrome, and I immediately thought of my beloved Scott at home. When I got home I told Scott, "Scott I met a man at the airport that had Down Syndrome." Scott's response was to touch my face and look deeply into my eyes and then he simply responded, "Ma, I know it!"

I do believe that Scott has a connection that we are all capable of having, but we are so busy and so caught up in our everyday lives that we miss it. I feel blessed in so many ways because Scott is in my life, and I truly believe he has come to teach me a valuable lesson: to love and accept and to value him first and foremost as the wonderful person that he is. Because of Scott I am able to do a job that I love, advocating for individuals with special needs; and I have met and made some of the best friends anyone could ask for. I am also at peace. I have experienced a spiritual side that was hidden from me until Scott showed me the way.

Barbara, a grandmother from Louisiana, wrote to tell me of her grandson, Elliot Andrew, and his encounters with angels.

I can only tell you that I have said from the time he was just a little fellow that I think he "talks to the angels." He plays in his room alone quite a bit when he is here visiting me, and I make frequent forays into "his space" to keep him grounded in "our world."

Often when I am about to enter his room, I stand outside his door and just listen. He is frequently standing before the full-length mirror on the back of the door, jabbering (in that language of autism those of us with autistic children all know) and frequently breaking into high-spirited giggling like he is enjoying a really good joke between him and whoever it is he is jabbering with. If I interrupt him "mid-conversation" he politely takes my hand, leads me to the door, opens it, leads me outside his room, reenters his room, says, "bye-bye" to me, closes the door, and goes right back to his "conversation." I think they appear to him (and him alone) in the mirror.

Sometimes he begins these conversations while I am already in the room with him. When that happens, he is suddenly, completely oblivious to me or my presence and quickly engages with whoever it is who "calls him." I am fascinated by it and think it is beautiful to watch. Of course, I suppose some folks would just say that I am putting a positive face onto a very negative behavior; however, I disagree. He is extremely happy and exhibits a beautiful countenance when his angels are visiting. He *much* prefers their company to that of us "mere earthlings." He is a very gentle soul and seems to personify the innocence combined with the bubbling joy of a cherubic soul.

PRIVATE COUNSEL

I have received many, many reports from others who have

validated this kind of activity—an individual with autism going off to be alone, usually the same environment at the same time of day, and having a two-way interaction with…someone unseen. Oftentimes, the person may laugh or smile during the interaction. One such affirmation came from Sabina, of southeast Missouri, writing about her young son with autism:

> I have witnessed on several occasions his conversations with someone that I could not see, and on occasion I could sense a presence during these conversations. I have also gotten comments from my son that are very profound and have strengthened my faith in God because I know in my heart that my son could not make these comments on his own; they have come from his personal experience and conversations with Him. It used to kind of disturb me, and I sometimes was afraid that my son was experiencing hallucinations or something, but now I embrace these things and in some ways envy my son for being able to remain so close to God. He is a nature lover and has taught me how to appreciate the world we live in again.

If you have observed or overheard something similar, please do not interrupt it or disservice the person by misinterpreting it as hallucinatory. Disbelievers will categorically dismiss such activity as senseless babble, the autistic equivalent of stereotypical "baby talk." My belief is that most often during these times the individual with autism is being privately *counseled* by a divine presence. The joy and laughter you may witness is an intentional respite provided to the individual in relief of what may be an extremely challenging life. Caroline, a mom from Richmond, Virginia, asserted that after such "sessions," her young son is so filled with pure joy that he actively seeks out others in order to "share" it by touching them lovingly—something he ordinarily would not do. Talk with caregivers of people at their most ethereal—those who are terminally ill, elderly, and dying—and you may learn of similar exaltations.

Maureen from Illinois specifically requested anonymity because of the brutally honest nature of her self-revelation. Her fears and anxieties were assuaged by her daughter's validating angel experience.

> My daughter is ten and she has autism. There have been many times throughout her life when I have wondered if she is clairvoyant or can read minds. There have been times when I have been thinking a question and she has answered verbally. There have been times when the phone or doorbell has rung and she said the person's name that was there (relatives she knew).
>
> There is one very particular instance I wish to relate. I am a single parent and at one point I was having a very difficult time spiritually. Now, looking back, I know I was very tempted to believe that I would sometime severely hurt my children, even though I rarely even spank. I was incredibly fearful and didn't trust myself. So every night I prayed a special prayer to St. Michael the Archangel to protect

us. [According to Scripture passages and Christian tradition, St. Michael the Archangel holds several offices including the fight against dark influences, and rescuing faithful souls from the power of the enemy.]

As my fears continued, I questioned whether we (especially my children) really were being protected.

One morning after waking, my daughter sat on the edge of the bed and looked out the window. After a minute she said, "Saint Michael the Archangel. What is St. Michael the Archangel doing there, mommy?" I looked and didn't see anything. But I suddenly knew this was the answer to my prayers. Almost precisely at that moment my fears of abusing my children left me and I was at peace. To this day (years later) I say that prayer every night, and I have never been tempted about such things again.

Jennifer's story is especially intriguing because of how her daughter, Megan, communicates. It is a validation of autism and the spiritual connection. She shared the following anecdote from her home in Minnesota.

I have a twelve-and-a-half-year-old daughter, Megan, diagnosed with autism. She is nonverbal and uses sign language to "talk." Just recently she informed me she saw a white girl with butterfly wings. She signed, "white," "girl," and "butterfly." I asked her did she mean that she saw wings, and my child's response was "yes." Since that first experience she has informed me that she has "seen white girl" again. The next three times she saw her "white girl" my daughter signed the exact same words in the exact same order to inform me she could see her. As she saw the girl her gaze every time has always been off to the left in an upward fashion. This came about immediately after being quite scared and having a need to be held. As I calmed her down and asked what was making her feel so scared she signed to me about the "white girl." Not knowing for sure if this was a good or bad thing I proceeded to ask her if the white girl was nice or bad to her. My daughter signed "nice, some bad." My gut instinct told me that my daughter was experiencing a paranormal experience, which would explain her initial fear.

The other interesting thing that occurred after the first visit was that very evening Megan asked for a necklace to wear. In fact she insisted! After several attempts to find the "right" one I came in with one with purple stones. Megan immediately wanted *that one*. She's not taken it off ever since. In her mind she was specific as to which one of mine she wanted to wear. It is a string necklace with purple stones tied by knots. Interestingly enough, once I put it on her she became *very calm* and appeared to be quite comforted. What little I know about the Spirit world and different colors having meaning, I already knew that purple is for protection.

It should also be noted that purple has long been associated with powerful properties and is used by bishops. It may denote sensitivity and spiritual understanding as well as personal or spiritual growth.

My most respectful speculation is that the white girl is indeed a spiritual entity that is pure and protective, and not at all harmful. It was natural that Megan was initially frightened by the entity's sudden appearance, hence her indecision as to whether she was "nice" or "bad." In the book *The Physics of Angels*, Dr. Matthew Fox, an Episcopal priest, describes angels as historically "awesome," and quotes the poet Rainer Maria Rilke who wrote that every angel is "terrifying." The appearance of angels in the Scriptures is usually accompanied by the words, "Do not be afraid." Fox continues, "Angels make human beings happy. It is rare to meet someone who has met an angel who doesn't wear a smile on his or her face. To encounter an angel is to return joyful," and further suggests, "Direct mental contact with these celestial entities may be possible through a kind of telepathy." (Of course this last statement makes complete sense in considering those individuals who do not speak, like Megan.)

Note that the white girl continues to visit Jennifer's daughter and that the aftereffects are no longer traumatic such that Megan reports them without fear. Jennifer confirmed my thinking in her follow-up message a few weeks later, in which she wrote:

> After the first experience I told Megan to tell the white girl with her thoughts, "Thank you for being here," and "Thank you to help me." Each time my daughter has these encounters she is more calmed now than the very first time. There also appears to be an essence of

peace within my child for a period of time.

Lori from Pennsylvania is ecstatic when talking about her angel:

> My angel is like my eyes. She sees everyone. She knows everyone. I see my angel every day. She lives with me. She is with me all of the time. My angel's name is Joy. She is pretty. She looks like me. She takes care of me. She makes me happy. She gives me love. She keeps me safe.

Angels are deemed as glorious messengers from the Creator. They are sacred intermediaries between Heaven and earth. Some of us may have experienced isolated encounters with an angelic deity in disguise, in dreams, or as a powerful vision. They are, perhaps, most readily discerned by those naturally predisposed to perceive them. As you've read, this includes individuals with different ways of being and autism.

Paying It Forward

To date, I have not had direct experience with angels, but, just like Mark Sachnik's observations, that's not to say that angelic influences weren't contributing to my journey. In assessing my life I realized I have never been seriously endangered, even in the times when I could have been. Nor have I had a serious illness, not even a broken bone. I also no longer saw things move out of the corner of my eye as I had in childhood. They were now directly in front of me, placed on top of my vision like an overhead projector transparency. I perceived the outlines of shapes moving through and beyond my range of vision. Sometimes it was significant enough to make me pause and think, "What was that?" Once while driving, such a shape passed before me, from right to left (which was really distracting). A second later, a driver in the next lane, crossing from right to left, came dangerously close to colliding with me.

By then I figured the responsible thing to do was to rule out any medical-related issues, so I endured exhaustive eye examinations and was seen by two different ophthalmologists, a technician, and a resident intern. I wear no corrective lenses and my ocular health is outstanding; in fact, my vision actually *improved* with age (I became near-sighted in school from burying my face in books in order to be invisible). In a test of my peripheral vision perception, done separately on each eye, I scored False Positive Errors of 2 percent and 1 percent, respectively. While the little cascading "globes" I regularly see are typical of many (called "floaters"), the doctors did not have a medical explanation for any of the above experiences.

As I grew and changed, I became a firm believer that you get back the energy you put out in the world. Many people with autism reflect back what others project upon them (hence my contention for the whole "making miracles" concept); however, I had been doing the reverse. I had been projecting indifference, insensitivity, and lack of real compassion for others. I'm living long enough to see what occurs when others are not mindful of this. Someone close to me can explode in ballistic temper. When it happens, I have witnessed household appliances malfunction in his hands, and, once, a computer became significantly scrambled through his attempts to use it as he normally would.

So, too, was I ascribing more value to my dreams. I began to comprehend the inherent symbolism. For example, to dream of someone profoundly doesn't necessarily mean they are imperiled or will soon die. Instead, it's a call to invest quality time in reconnecting while they are still here to enjoy. I understood this most clearly the morning after a dream in which I embraced my dear grandmother and told her with childish naïveté, "I've loved you ever since I was a little boy." As she rocked me in her arms, the scene around us changed from her basement to an endless vista of beautiful, golden wheat fields with people contentedly harvesting the grain. Upon awakening, I was certain the dream was prophetic of her having just passed, and I called her as soon as I could. Imagine my anxiety when she took longer than usual to answer the phone! She was touched when I shared the dream. I have since made the effort to call her weekly, and once a month I bring her flowers and take her to lunch.

Conversely, a dream I had about a man with Down Syndrome, with whom I had previously worked, left me feeling happy and full of affection. Shortly afterward, I learned he had passed away a few years back. He returns to me regularly in dreams, always filled with adoration for me.

The White Horse Returns

The white horse has appeared only one other time in a dream, within a month after the first dream. On Thanksgiving break, I traveled to New York State to spend the holiday with immediate and extended family, some of whom I had never met. I knew that one cousin had a young boy with autism, and I so wanted to approach the family to make myself available if they so desired. But I didn't know *how* to enter into such a situation without seeming presumptuous during a highly distractible time for everyone. I couldn't just introduce myself and say, "Oh, by the way, I just want to let you know I'm an autism consultant," a social faux pas I would've committed at one time. I struggled with this after the first day, knowing that I would have limited opportunities to make a connection. That night, I had a dream that foretold, symbolically, exactly how it would transpire.

In the dream, I observed from above, a large square field covered with light snow (there was actually snow already on the ground where we were in real time). In the lower right corner of the square field I saw the boy in question crawling and beginning to make his way into the field from outside it. I next observed the white horse, wingless this time, at the topmost edge of the field. The horse trotted out of the field and began to run toward the left alongside the top edge of the field, round the corner, and proceed down the left side of the field. It was not running *in* the field but on the black macadam of a road that followed the square perimeter of the field. Its hooves sounded thunderous on the pavement. Meanwhile, the boy had about made his way just inside the lower right corner of the field. At this time, the horse had traveled down the length of the left side of the field and was now proceeding along the bottom edge of the field, headed toward the area where the boy was. And…I woke up, dream over.

I knew the dream held significance because I was reminded that the horse represented me. The location was not unlike any number of snow-covered fields near us, and this was a specific little boy I had only just met hours earlier. I equated it all with my immediate surroundings and circumstance. What I didn't know was how it all added up. I was to soon find out.

The next evening, everyone planned to convene for an anniversary dinner at a local restaurant. The family had reserved most of a big back room for the event, and the tables were arranged in a large, square horseshoe shape. After some debate, I sat at the bottom edge. The cousin and his family sat on either side of the tables next to me and up the right edge of the adjoining tables. The cousin's wife sat next to me, and we chatted. While discussing her young son, we entered into a conversation about the true beauty of autism. The conversation bonded us and brought us both to tears. I then realized the inevitable. My position at the outside table was precisely where the white horse had stopped running as my dream ended. The boy was seated *inside* the square, just beyond the lower right edge and exactly where he had been in the dream!

Now it all made sense except for one detail that took some time for me to process: why hadn't the horse simply connected with the boy by taking the shortcut and running diagonally across the field to meet him where he was? The answer was the same as my rationale that it was in poor taste to conspicuously introduce myself as an autism consultant. There was a gentler, more natural way in. And, knowing how exquisitely sensitive some people's hearing can be, the horse made the best choice by running around the perimeter of the field, ensuring that its hooves rang out on the pavement instead of muffled by the grass and snow. This way, the boy would not be startled, could hear the horse in the distance, and could have time to prepare for its arrival.

MENTORING DREAMS

By this time, I felt like I was being systematically prepared for "something" by a Higher Power, although I knew not what. I now had vivid, nightly dreams in which people sought me to minister to them. In one dream, a man asked to be healed. In another, I understood that a simple problem would not be resolved by anyone on my behalf; there was an obstacle from which to learn. In this case, it seemed trivial: how to preserve a carton of milk (i.e., nourishment) outdoors until it was needed for a family's meal. After I found a viable solution (asking a nearby workman to keep it in his lunch cooler), I next had to smooth over the rift caused within the family. The dream was a symbolic way of communicating an essential concept. There are circumstances imposed upon our lives deliberately that contribute to our self-growth and education.

Other dreams were a series of lessons, realistic opportunities to temporarily "live" various experiences. These included opening a nightstand drawer merely by thinking of its contents; knowing of the grotesque and humiliating things people will do to one another or themselves under duress or for money (think *Jerry Springer* on a far more aberrant level); comprehending religious fanaticism; counseling other souls on the educational virtues of incarnating as one who is paraplegic; sensing a duality, that there existed another half of "me;" or understanding how to fly by running in the same direction that the wheat bowed in the wind. (In another similar flying dream, I quickly realized that soaring Superman-style was impractical; maintaining my outstretched arms against the centrifugal force was exhausting and, quite simply, not aerodynamic.)

I also awoke from a dream one morning realizing that I had just resolved a conflict from a perspective that was a unique and previously inexperienced way of thinking. One night, I knew I had a long series of dreams but, upon awakening, couldn't retrieve details of any of them; I was, though, left with the distinct impression to stay true to what is kind and loving. In another dream, everything around me was coming undone. Despite my distress, the message I received was to stay bonded in God, as that was all that really mattered.

In another significant dream, I was in the home of a family familiar to me, but the child with autism was unfamiliar. He was small with dark hair cut in bangs across his forehead. His gentle face featured large brown, earnest-looking eyes. I assumed that he was a composite of many similar boys I knew. In the dream, the boy's slightly older brother accidentally brushed against him while the boy and I were engaged in conversation. The boy suddenly, physically lashed out at his brother, not realizing his own strength. The brother yelped in pain, and clutched himself as he doubled over. In spite of his brother's wailing, I asked the boy if there was anything he could do. Was there some way he could take back, or "absorb" the pain on his brother's behalf for what had been an accidental slight? As the brother's cries ceased, the boy went limp in my arms, completely drained until my shaking and calling revived him.

I knew that Native Americans historically honored persons with disabilities as mystics and respected them for their ability to heal among other gifts; but here was the inkling of something I hadn't even begun to consider where autism was involved.

PRAYER AND HEALING

The intent of healing oneself or others through prayer or meditation is yet another area that has recently received the attention of scientific research at preeminent institutions such as the Mind/Body Institute of Massachusetts, Duke University Medical Center, North Carolina, and San Francisco's California Pacific Medical Center. A 2004 survey of 31,000 people by the CDC showed that 43 percent of adults in the U.S. prayed for their own health and 24 percent prayed for the health of others. Spurred by such encouraging statistics, the National Institutes of Health's National Center for Complementary and Alternative Medicine has, since 2000, invested over $2 million studying healing through prayer. Similarly, Petaluma's Institute of Noetic Sciences (IONS), founded by former astronaut Edgar Mitchell, has as its mission the exploration of "phenomena that do not necessarily fit conventional scientific models." Among those defending the scientific investigation of healing is Dr. Marilyn Schlitz, vice president of research and education at IONS and senior scientist at California Pacific Medical Center. Dr. Schlitz's work examines whether the human mind has hidden capacities that promote healing. She contends, "The survey data is saying people pray, that they are using it as part of their healing regimen. Shouldn't science look at that? Maybe it helps in certain kinds of conditions and not in others. Well, we cannot answer that unless we take a vigorous, systematic look at what people are actually doing."

I wondered, were certain persons with autism of such divine influence that they, too, possessed a natural proclivity for healing? Was such an empathic feat possible in real time? During one visit with my friend Kevin (mentioned earlier in this chapter), he was seemingly agitated, up and circling around those of us seated at the kitchen table. Suddenly he struck out and "karate-chopped" my colleague Craig. Everyone interpreted this as an act of physical aggression because, well, that's what it looked like. But what Craig confided on the drive home was that he had had a painful kink in his shoulder and—somehow—Kevin had hit him in the same bothersome spot with deft precision (not actually striking him as hard as it looked). Kevin's darting jab relieved the knotted muscle that had been causing Craig significant discomfort. Coincidence or Kevin's capacity for intuitive empathy?

By extension, allow me to dispel another stereotype about people with autism or Asperger's Syndrome. The stereotype suggests that most lack the ability to feel sensitivity or empathy for others. Yet those with autism are the most gentle and compassionate people I know. (By contrast I've found many are not terribly concerned with the false realities of earthly contrivances such as physical beauty, wealth, or material possessions.) Many families and caregivers can attest to the generous, loving connections they enjoy as the recipients of great affection. One friend with autism became visibly upset when he accurately foresaw two separate car accidents involving loved ones with whom he was deeply attached before anyone informed him. The circumstances of my dream about the boy and his injured brother did not seem so implausible to me. In fact, English philosopher and novelist, Charles Williams, believed the highest form of love was to take on another's suffering as an act of substitution.

This principle appears to be the underlying motivation for the connection made by young Elena and her unsuspecting benefactor. Her mother, Ziek, told me from her New York City home:

> Elena is considered "low-functioning" autistic. She is nonverbal and unable to "do" anything without full assistance. Since she learned to walk independently at age eight, she would find her way through a gathering of people, patting a butt or tugging a shirt sleeve and making "connections" with a remarkable capacity for choosing people who would smile and offer a loving response and often have a story to share of a nephew or cousin who is autistic as well. One story in particular, of hundreds of examples, comes to mind. In this case, however, her contact was not immediately so well received. Once, after a worship service, there was a fairly large crowd and a fellowship hour that followed. Elena made her way through the crowd as usual—her little "ambassador" self. I tend to monitor her from a distance, giving her space to do her "work" and to meet people on her own terms. I just watch out that she doesn't get hurt or get into the food, which could prove quite disastrous. This one time I watched from behind as Elena walked up and stood next to an elderly man while he was engaged in conversation with another man, who was standing with his back a few feet from a

wall. Neither man seemed to notice her there. After a moment she slipped her hand into that of the elderly man, who looked down at her and carefully, using his free hand, disengaged his hand from hers and continued his conversation, ignoring her. She stood there beside him for a few moments as the two men finished their conversation, and the second man walked off. At that moment Elena slipped her hand back into that of the elderly man.

By this time I was coming around from the side slowly, evaluating the possible need for my intervention. As I approached, he was allowing her hand in his, and I noticed that he had tears welling up in his eyes, as he stood there facing the wall. I came closer and he connected that I was her mother. He asked me softly, "What is her name?" to which I answered, "Elena." At that moment his tears began to flow freely. After a half a minute or so, still holding her hand, he told me, "Today is the anniversary of my wife's death." He paused as I gave him a heartfelt look of compassion. And then he continued, "Her name was Elena." I felt clearly that there was tremendous healing for him in this wordless child holding his hand and his tears flowing freely for the loss of his beloved wife. My sense was (and is) that there was great grief being released in those tears.

People sometimes ask me if Elena has any particular skill or ability (like a savant quality) and I tell them, "Yes, she is a heart savant. She opens people's hearts!"

My own acts of substitution spilled forth in the body of my work. There's a saying, "Do what you are." I work purely by intuition, drawing from my own personal experiences as an individual with Asperger's, and the experiences of others. I've learned to wholeheartedly trust my instincts, and they've *never* failed me. I am tremendously humbled and fortunate to do this work for a living. It is a great privilege and an honor, and I don't take it any of it for granted—not for a moment. Because in the moment that occurs, it could all be taken away just as quickly.

I now approach life with a sense of wonder and anticipation as events unfold before me like a movie. I can interpret life objectively from an outsider's perspective. From this vantage point, I'm in a better position to consider, "What am I supposed to be learning from this?" Every day, and especially before going into a consultation or workshop, I ask that the Universe use me as the tool through which to communicate sensitive, humanistic messages. Because of years of damaged self-esteem, it is difficult for me to gracefully accept compliments. This is magnified when people praise me for my work. But I am unable to fully accept credit because the Creator uses me as a vessel. My usual reply is one that others have heard me say countless times, "It doesn't come *from* me, it comes *through* me."

Validations

six

Izzy

❧

Springtime 2003, I found myself lodged in a quaint road-side inn preparing for a presentation as ivory cherry blossoms scattered in the breeze outside my door in fine imitation of an April snow shower. At 7:30 a.m. it was already a beautiful morning but little did I know just how momentous a day it would be, for, very soon, I would have the privilege of making Izzy's acquaintance.

Izzy's mother, Roz, and older sister, Deb, were among the roomful of folks who filed into the community room of the local library an hour later to register for my two-day autism seminar. With everyone in place, I walked to the podium and began to set the tone for our time together, espousing many of the same philosophies of respect and reverence found in this text. Soon after the start of the presentation, Deb raised her hand and meekly asked if I knew anything about people with autism "predicting things." Preferring to build from smallest to largest, and being too early in the discussion to jump directly to largest (at least *that* kind of largest), I tactfully sidestepped Deb's question. Still, I was feeling a bit duplicitous, having left Deb hanging without resolve to her honest inquiry—an inquiry I knew I was poised to answer.

At the first break, I approached both Roz and Deb and got to chatting with them as discreetly as possible because others were nearby socializing, sipping yet another coffee, and generally milling about. In as much as a fifteen-minute break would allow, the women told me about their beloved Izzy and his intuitive abilities to inherently "know" what someone was thinking and feeling. As our mutual comfort level quickly grew, Roz and Deb began to share information about Izzy's remarkable gifts in greater depth. I was fascinated and enthusiastic: never before had I met anyone with autism who sounded so wise and authentic. They committed to adjusting schedules and slipping Izzy out of his day program the following morning in order to briefly meet me. I was so intrigued I could hardly wait for the next day. That night, I sat on a lawn chair outside my rented room, half-distracted by the continuous rain of cherry blossoms, and pondered autism, the universe, and everything.

I awoke with keen anticipation the following morning, undaunted even by the flower petals that had conspired to silently polka dot my car during the night; just as quietly, I cleared a dewy swath on my windshield before heading out. Once there, I stood in the parking lot outside the library awaiting Izzy's arrival, quietly nervous but full of spiritual optimism. It wasn't long before Roz's car pulled up, and she and Deb and Izzy piled out. Making carefully measured steps along the asphalt, Izzy walked right to me, and I took his delicate hand in mine—as white as the generous cherry blossoms—and we gazed upon one another for the first time. It was then that Izzy and I began a relationship; he even told his sister he knew what I would look like before meeting me. It was an auspicious beginning and I, the eager student, readily yielded to Izzy's stewardship.

At twenty-six, Izzy resembles a reclining Buddha: large and round and soft with closely cropped hair and an inner sense of mirth and wisdom. His eyes are icy-azure and ever-clear; his flesh, alabaster. Up until two years prior, he had been diagnosed as severely mentally retarded, unable to communicate except for some lilting verbalizations and, occasionally, an isolated word or two. Izzy and his family found blessed liberation through learning about Facilitated Communication and introducing it to him. He became fluent in no time, typing some words independently and making a believer out of a skeptical psychologist. Deb asserted that Izzy's proclivity for using this mode of communication "has changed all of our lives."

As a result of our meeting that day, Izzy and I struck up a regular email correspondence. Deb and Roz would visit him every day in his group home to share my most recent communications; Izzy would type his replies, and Deb would transcribe them back to me at night. By late May, Izzy became disconcerted by the appearance of angels communicating to him. He wrote to his mother of the comfort he received from his father's Spirit. (Grammar and misspellings are unedited. Please note Izzy's "shorthand" such as spelling the word "know" as "no," or "you" as "u.")

> I feel better today. I was nervous yesterday mom. U are not going to believe what i have to say mom. Dad came to me last night. He wanted me to see my

angels at my side. He wanted me to not be afraid. He
told me they watch over me. I now understand. I am
seeing things different now. i no i am put on earth for
all time just to learn about life. i had to be like i am
so i dont lose focus in my being here mom. i here just
a short time. i no u no that mom. God is nice. He will
always prevail in doing good for humanity mom.

Izzy later revealed that one angel in particular, named
Francine, is a special protector. She is fun loving and offsets
the seriousness of Izzy's Spirit Guide. Izzy told me that his
angel's name is the same as what his sister's used to be. Deb
was astounded and wrote, "When I was born my mom
named me Francine, but due to an aunt of mine complaining
she didn't like the name and really harping on it, my mom
changed my name before she brought me home from the
hospital. I knew this. My mom had told me when I was very
small. There is no way in the world Izzy or either of my other
brothers would know this."

Izzy was also gracious and forthcoming in sharing his spiritual thoughts with me for the purpose of including them in
this book. He wrote:

Tell Bill i am learning a lot from my faith. Fill my heart
with live. I see my ancestors who passed before me.
I no i can feel things that only God would no about
them. i am sure of this. i feel my famly is safe in Gods
Heavens. i feel i see my family that even my mom
dont no. i see a lot of things about people here on
earth. People are very superficial. they only care

about themselfs. . God not like people like that. He wants to make people happy, learn things on earth. i learned lots of things so far. I learned u don't have to be perfect to be loved. My mom love for me is so great. i so very lucky she visited me ever day, has faith in me. No i can see Gods hand on me when i get scared. i very lucky i have a mom who believes in me. she understands my problems, whats to learn about how i think and feel. i can tell her anything.

mom tell Bill if he can use any of this i would be honored to share my feelings with them. i just average man with autism. If u looked at me u think i am dumb. i make noises, sometimes i shake, get stuck, sometimes to, but i very lucky. i can feel God always helps me to be a good person. i understand i not the smartest man here , but i try to learn so when i go to my God i try to bring him some of life experiences to maybe help somebody else when they come to earth and may have problems here, it can be easier for them to cope wth it. i no mad i was born with problems. i just lucky i had parents who cared and loved me…Godbless u.

Izzy further recalled details of his difficult entry into this world, and prior to his birth. He requested that Deb contact me to relay his memories:

Izzy said he remembers that the cord was wrapped around his neck and he said every time he went down into the birth canal it strangled him. He said this kept happening but he knew that he had to be born. When he was born, he was born stillborn (his words); he wasn't breathing, but he said he knew he had to live. The doctor did bring him back.

Bill, this is all true—there is absolutely no way he could have known any of it since we never talked about it, there is no way he could have heard it. The above is all Izzy's words.

My mom asked him if he knew what day of the week he was born. He knew—he was born Easter Monday in the morning. This is another thing that we never discussed. There really was never any reason to discuss it, but he knew it. Izzy also said he knew my mom had a C-section, which was absolutely right. The doctor had to do that since he kept climbing back up the birth canal, but there really is no explainable way Izzy could know any of that—this is nothing my mom would have discussed. I knew it because I could remember right after Izzy was born, but this was nothing that was ever talked about since then at all. So his memory has to be accurate from that time.

In another amazing instance, Izzy already knew what I had written *without seeing it*. Deb was enduring a bout of the flu and didn't make one of the daily visits. I had emailed her with questions for Izzy, asking for his insights about a dream I had in which I purchased four small books in a gift shop. Deb intended that Roz would stop by to pick up a printout of my email for Izzy, but that didn't happen. Instead, when Roz met with Izzy, he began to type his response, specifically addressing

details of my dream. Izzy said that the four books represented compass directions: north, south, east, west. He went on
to further interpret the dream in answer to questions I had
wondered in my message to him. Neither Roz nor Izzy had
this information in advance. It was a brilliant demonstration
of his God-given gift.

I later had a dream in which the colors red and gold were
prominent. When I shared this with Izzy, he succinctly
informed me that red and gold are "God's light colors." Red
is the color of the blood Christ shed for us, and gold represents God's purity. Shortly thereafter, Izzy's pastor used his
contemplations about "God's light colors" in a sermon.

On one pilgrimage to sit with Izzy in his group home, I
asked him who he was before this life. He blue eyes flashed
and he seemed a bit surprised that I posed the question. He
wrote:

Yes Bill u first person to ask me…I remember being
in Heaven before I was born, no body, just spirit.
God's love great, beautiful there. I no i special. I no i
have hard job to do here. People not believe, really
believe. I try hard, but not being able to speak, I
depend on other people. I no u believe in me. I smart
man foget my body, speech. I try to relay my deep
feelings about God. Not everyone believes in me. I
try God tells me I doing what I was put on earth to do.

I was a priest in the thirteenth centry. Not everyone listened to me, afraid i was devil, would hurt
them. Tried to show God's love. They only believe
in rulers. I was killed by guards of bad man. I was

> stabbed by long saber. My name is hard to say. I not
> good speller. Russia. I not sure, think I was in Heaven
> long time.

During another one of our get-togethers, Izzy so eloquently summarized his earthly mission as a person with autism. As is true of all his quotes presented here, he has given consent for his words to be reproduced for all to see. He wrote:

> I can feel strong love more than seeing. Do u under-
> stand? I understand Bill. My love is very strong. I feel
> God with me all the time. I only feel his great love.
> My heart is love. I think I told u if i had choice
> between normal or my love for God, God wins big
> time. I don't think of my body. I try only to think of
> love, God's love.
>
> Bill stay with what u doing, don't get discouraged.
> I no it's hard, but remember me. I didnt do anything
> for 23 years, and now look, so if u feel dead and keep
> going that's u mission. Yes, it's hard, but look at me,
> talking to u, but making noises. People say nothing is
> here, but there is Bill.

These are indeed powerful, thought-provoking sentiments from a divine and exquisitely sensitive human being—some-one for whom, previously, others had not presumed intellect. I wonder how many like Izzy are out there, patiently await-ing the opportunity to spiritually mentor us all for the greater good. How privileged we might be for it. Izzy seems to have the ability to straddle two worlds, with the capacity to distill the essence of what he perceives of a Heavenly realm. His experiences, and the communications of his father in Spirit, validated an experience of my own that occurred the autumn before he and I both met.

GRAMPA

As I was getting ready for a doctor's appointment the morning of October 28, 2002, I found myself thinking about my grandfather, realizing that his birthday was Halloween. I didn't often think of him. I didn't know him very well and have precious few memories of him. While waiting for the doctor to come into my patient room, I was trying to find something to read, and was sorting through magazines. The top of a *Newsweek* that peeked out from the wall rack carried a headline about newly discovered photos of Marilyn Monroe, which sounded interesting. But as I pulled it out completely I saw the cover story was titled "Visions of Heaven" with a large Italian Renaissance painting of angels and cherubs lifting some soul Heavenward. Not surprisingly, the article compared our "ideal" of Heaven to the Land of Oz (Oz references in my readings have been ubiquitous).

The doctor was pleased with my recovery from back pain, which I attributed to a combination of time, medication, and prayer. Upon leaving, I began writing my check for the insurance copay and looked at my watch to write the date. Inexplicably, the date had somehow *jumped ahead* several days and my watch now showed October 31—Grampa's birthday! Although the date had changed, the actual time was still accurate. I was stunned, and even commented to the receptionist. I'd had the battery-powered watch for nearly ten years and never encountered this before. As I could not reverse wind it back to 28, I had to manually wind it forward until I could reset it. (A local, experienced jeweler with working knowledge of my watch brand had never heard of such a thing.) In the following days, I periodically checked it for malfunctions but it ran just fine.

The night my watch jumped ahead, I had a strong dream from which I awoke feeling as though I'd glimpsed the Other Side, perhaps courtesy of my grandfather (not unlike Izzy's experiences with his father's Spirit). In the dream, I was on the edge of a beautiful meadow leading to a wooded area that graduated into a forest, rich and earthy. It was all so familiar, that I felt I had been there once before. As I journeyed along uphill, a photograph from *The Wizard of Oz* that I had been holding blew out of my hand and off the path. It fluttered down a verdant valley that led to a spectacular waterfall, which emptied into a shallow stream. The photograph symbolized the one earthly passion that would be difficult for me to ever surrender and release (at least at the time).

I followed the photograph, but was able to allow it to remain in favor of being drawn closer to the breathtaking waterfall area. It was so vivid that I could experience the sensation of being one with the water; its effervescence crackled in my mouth like the tang of seltzer. Everything felt more alive including the air in my nostrils.

But since I veered off the main path, distracted by the photograph, I now had to continue the journey by crossing the stream. Smooth and glistening flat rocks and stones lay above the water's surface such that crossing the stream would not present any great challenge. But there was some apprehension

because a strong light fell across a portion of the area I needed to cross, which would cause me to be unable to see my
way. The sense I got was "trust," trust that I could cross safely to the other side of the stream. Then I might take my place
in a higher area, on a hillside above the stream that butted
against an auditorium. It was another test, and as I reached
my destination, I awakened.

Several weeks later I came upon a passage in Dr. Raymond
Moody's book, *The Light Beyond*, in which sixth-century
pope Gregory the Great's *Dialogues* is quoted. Moody contends it is the first historical documentation of "life after life."
In the account, a soldier overcome by the plague is said to
have described similar circumstances during an out-of-body
experience. As he was drawn out of his body, he found himself before a bridge under which ran black and noxious
waters. But beyond laid lush meadows carpeted with green
grass and perfumed with flowers. The account continues
(italics are my emphasis): "On the bridge there was a *test*. If
any unjust person wished to cross, he slipped and fell into the
black and stinking water. But the just, who were not blocked
by guilt, *freely and easily made their way across* to the region of
delight."

I spent the day before my grandfather's birthday with my
Gramma. In part we looked at old family slides. Even though
some were well over fifty years old, their Kodachrome hues
were vibrant and alive. Many of them featured images of
Grampa, and we both agreed it was a loving way to pay him
tribute at his birthday.

When I shared this experience with Izzy, he was serene in
assuring me that, while I may have glimpsed the outskirts of

the Other Side, Heaven was far more exquisite and dazzling than anything I had perceived. Izzy's consistent and unwavering messages of staying bonded in love resonated whenever I reflected upon this revelation of my own. I would strive to preserve those impressions in my future relationships with others.

seven

Ghosts in the Laboratory

&

Of all the alarming national news stories about autism and abuse, perhaps none have created such uproar as those in which children with autism were deemed "possessed." An August 2003 incident made headlines when an eight-year-old boy was restrained and suffocated during an exorcism ceremony at a Milwaukee strip-mall church. The church's bishop justified his actions stating, "We were asking God to take this spirit that was tormenting this little boy to death. We were praying that hard, but not to kill." (Those with epilepsy and Tourette's Syndrome were once identically perceived.) One might think such a radical formality as exorcism would be exempt as an option in this day and age given what we are learning about autism. But this case shows how very blurred the lines can become between parental desperation, best intentions, religious influence, and inexcusable ignorance.

Like my earliest encounter with Kyle, I became embroiled in another situation—albeit an extreme instance—in which an individual with autism may have been at great risk of being labeled psychotic or even possessed had his experience not been validated by others. It is a cautionary tale that implores us not to jump to conclusions but to be thorough in exploring all possibilities, exhausting all avenues, and truly listening to what someone is telling us. Remember, often-times the person with autism is so very literal in what they interpret and communicate.

At the onset of winter 2003, I had been asked to consult with a team supporting a twenty-one-year-old young man with autism named Josh. Josh is well over six-feet tall and rail thin with piercing blue eyes, short red-gold hair, and elegant, refined features. So sensitive is he, that if Josh wears anything other than cotton against his skin, he breaks out into red welts. Josh resided in a residential school for children with autism and had lived there for the past ten years; but because he was no longer of school age, Josh was not eligible to continue receiving services at the school and needed to transition to another living arrangement. It was decided that he would move across the state and return to his home county, where his family still lived. I led Josh's parents, school team, and receiving professionals in thoroughly assessing all facets of his life; we created a plan of support for Josh in order to meet his hopes, needs, dreams, and desires.

As part of my services to Josh's team, I trained them in using Facilitated Communication in advance of his move because Josh does not speak fluently. Josh presently used FC with his mother and had used it at the school initially; but it was dropped there early in his tenure in favor of using a picture system, which Josh refused. Paper keyboards were now plastered around Josh's new house and his staff was prepared to engage him when he was ready.

Also prior to Josh's move, I conducted an environmental assessment of the house that had been selected as most suitable for him. It was a brick, ranch-style home built in the 1960s and positioned on a rural hillside but sandwiched between two highways. I liked the home very much, especially for its hardwood floors and woodsy setting. Josh would have his own bedroom and would share the house with another man (without autism), already living there. I soon learned that the house was nicknamed "Laboratory," after its address, Laboratory Lane.

Josh had been living there a few weeks when he began to have trouble sleeping during the night. Shortly after Josh moved in, I presented an autism sensitivity training for his staff. It was at this training that they raised their concerns for Josh. When one staff member had asked Josh what was upsetting him, Josh had typed the word "ghost." They wanted to know what this meant and what they should do about it. From our previous assessment of Josh's records, his current psychiatric status, and interviews with family and staff, we knew there were no outstanding mental health issues. So, we entered into a dialogue explaining how exquisitely sensitive some people with autism can be in perceiving things others do not. We followed that up by acknowledging their responsibility to not sensationalize what Josh was reporting, to keep it confidential, and to accept what he was telling them as the truth. They agreed to do so and would continue offering him their assurances that everything was okay.

But everything was not okay, and after about a month, Josh couldn't get through a night without waking up screaming, rushing down the hallway and, on occasion, grabbing staff around the throat. When he was calm, Josh would type that there was no longer one ghost in his bedroom but several. And he was naming them. Samuel was twenty-one, and was the first to keep him up all night; Edward was a bearded man. Another was named Sarah. And a "woman" had taken up residence in the spare room across the hall. Josh indicated that, in all, there were five of them, and they were originating from the small cemetery that was adjacent to the property. (In my assessment of the house, I had never seen the graveyard, which was very small and hidden behind some trees.) Remarkably, when staff checked the names Josh had given them against the 1800s-era cemetery headstones, they *matched* even though Josh was always within the sight of his staff and had never been in the graveyard. Specifically, there was a Samuel who had died at age twenty-one.

With each passing week, the situation seemed to deteriorate as the entities set up root in the house. Now their number had jumped to nine according to Josh, and things were beginning to manifest in real time. One night a staff person heard a little girl talking and giggling in Josh's room; someone else glimpsed her reflection in a window. Another person was preparing a snack of cookies and orange slices, set out on separate platters. Upon returning to the room, the foods were all mixed together. On another occasion, a staff person went into the basement office to retrieve a stack of papers from the desk of a locked room. Instead of being where they should've been, the papers were now scattered to the other side of the room. Two others saw green flashing lights in Josh's room that were not outside reflections. Intermittent blasts of cold air were felt. Most dramatically, in two photographs taken of

Josh, the face of a bearded man could be clearly seen hovering in the air at floor level; when digitally enlarged on a television screen, its features were distinct.

Amy, Josh's case manager, called me in desperation. Josh's mental and physical health was being significantly compromised and, while his staff was hanging in there, they were understandably freaked out, and one person had already quit. The more I heard, the angrier I got. It was clear to me that Josh was the innocent in all this, and I was upset that he was being taken advantage of. His sensitivity was being used as a "way in" for the others. That is, his elevated frequency was the conduit or conductor that they rode in on. This did not seem entirely improbable to me; one mom whom I interviewed told me that her son was at risk of being mislabeled with mental health issues because of his inappropriate "behaviors," which ranged from spontaneous mirth to mortification, until he conceded he was picking up radio frequencies and reacting to the broadcasts. This was verified when the family confirmed his news reports.

Amy next confided to me that she was very sensitive herself, and, as a child, could see Spirits. In fact, Josh had recently typed with her, "U C ghosts," indicating that he could perceive this about her as well. We made a plan to visit Laboratory when I was next in town in a couple weeks. Amy would clear everything with Josh's agency so that everyone in the house could take a ride while we attempted to "clean house" by praying and firmly telling the entities to release their hold on Josh. It was ambitious and possibly dangerous but, other than having the house formally blessed, I didn't have any fast and easy solutions.

You may be wondering where Josh's parents were in all this. Both have longstanding, solid reputations in their community as staunch advocates, not only for their son but on behalf of the children of others. They were also witness to several of the very unusual incidents that occurred in Josh's house, and they are open-minded enough to discern that the forces influencing their son were external and not the internal workings of autism stereotypes or mental illness. Nor were there any conspiracies contrived to unhinge Josh. His staff is a dedicated and caring group of people. Josh, himself, did not deliberately concoct a ruse either; it was, for all intents and purposes, quite real to everyone concerned.

A couple Sundays before Amy's call, I saw Josh and his parents at a meeting. Josh was gaunt and tired and extremely agitated as well. My heart broke for him. In talking with Josh, he didn't realize that he had the authority to resist the presences plaguing him. He didn't realize saying "no" was an option and he agreed to try. Later, when I had the chance to privately interview Josh again (with his mother supporting him to type), I asked him if he knew what the presences wanted. He replied that he didn't know because they "talk too fast." This is consistent with the high-pitched frequency "chatter" from Spirits described by some spiritualists.

My friend Izzy was also at the same meeting. Izzy shared his empathy with Josh and advised that Josh have faith in God. After Josh left, Izzy's concern lingered. He asked his mother Roz to give me money to buy Josh a statue of a saint. When I asked which one, Izzy typed, "St. Patrick. He's good at looking out for kids." Roz handed me a twenty-dollar bill, and I pledged to try finding Josh a St. Patrick statue for my impending visit.

Just before leaving home for my trip to see Josh, Amy called again. She had been talking to a staff member named Jerry about what was happening for Josh and how anxious everyone was feeling. Jerry told Amy that his mom, Delores, had been very sensitive all her life. Amy and Delores got in touch with one another and hit it off. They went out to the house together and walked in the tiny graveyard. Given her accuracy, Amy thought it best if Delores accompanied us on our visit. I was glad for the added support and welcomed Delores' wisdom. The three of us combined would be a powerful force.

When I got into town, I heard from Amy again. Delores wanted to meet and her daughter, Carolyn, wanted to come along too. What I learned was that Carolyn was also gifted and, since early childhood, had the ability to see Spirits. For a time, Carolyn blocked it out as too unnerving, but she was beginning to open herself to the visions once more.

We got together that same evening and met in my hotel room to craft a plan. I immediately took to Delores. She was about sixty, full-figured with dark hair and black eyes that radiated warmth. She was like granite, solid in her sense of self and in her gifts to aid others. She had found missing children for the FBI, and some years back, she had given her husband, then a New York City cop, tips that proved accurate in the capture of David "Son of Sam" Berkowitz. Carolyn was a very young-looking forty-one, demure, and soft-spoken.

Dialoguing with them, I was still in irritation mode and my first allegiance was protecting Josh. After all, the presences were stuck clinging to the 1800s—didn't that make us more progressive and wiser than they were? By the same token, I wanted to be helpful to them if at all possible. Delores was able to temper my feelings. Her sense was that, in order to alleviate Josh's angst, we had to determine what the presences wanted. She and Amy had been doing some local research. The markers in the graveyard represented two different families. The dates on them were from the early to mid-1800s. What they learned was that a number of family members died from tuberculosis. The two women also got the sense that there was a murder or suicide—at the least someone died from something other than natural causes. We decided that, the following evening, we would walk through the cemetery, walk the grounds, and then survey the house room by room. We would adopt an attitude that was open and diplomatic but firm and determined. We all joined hands in prayer before parting that night.

Throughout our discussion, Carolyn took notes but was mostly silent and sometimes seemed distracted. What I learned from Amy the next day was that Carolyn had seen a figure cloaked in a white veil standing behind me. She knew it was a benevolent, protective presence intended for me. I wept. At this point, not knowing what we were up against, I welcomed all the help I could get. With as aggressive and out of control as things had become, I anticipated some kind of confrontation. That night I slept fitfully, my mind preoccupied with a million unanswered questions that refused to be assuaged.

The following day, Amy and I met about an hour before our trip. I was still on a mission to find Josh the St. Patrick statue that Izzy directed me to purchase. Amy was only aware of one such religious store in the area and we decided to stop there before driving on to Josh's house. I figured if St. Patrick wasn't to be found, I'd simply turn the twenty dollars over to Josh's parents and ask that they take the lead from there. We got out of the car and entered a building that essentially looked like a Goodwill thrift shop had exploded—junk was piled and scattered everywhere. Surreptitiously inching along the obstacle-course aisles, we saw many things but no figurines of any kind. Just to be certain, I finally inquired and a clerk redirected us to a showcase we apparently passed at the front of the store; any keepsake figures would be there. Amy and I wended our way back through the clutter toward the showcase, an old department store cast-off. We quickly discovered that the shop had just one statue of one saint priced at exactly twenty dollars. Sure enough, silently awaiting us was St. Patrick, resplendent in his flowing green robes and mild-mannered countenance. It was a good sign.

The sky was darkening as we headed back down the highway en route for the hour-long trek to the house. Amy and I would meet Delores and Carolyn there. I was a bit apprehensive but had been praying for guidance and support. In my mind, Josh's well being came first, my personal concerns were secondary.

Pulling up the steep, winding driveway, I fully expected to experience an ominous or foreboding sensation. I didn't. Instead, I felt strong and confident. The house looked just as it always had, and I sensed nothing untoward. But when I walked inside, I found Josh literally bouncing off the walls with nervous anxiety. Various staff members tried to engage him in FC, but he was too agitated to focus. Finally, he sat with me and began to calm. He started by typing standard small talk, "Hi Bill. How are you?" Then he cut to the chase, "Love me as you love Christ." I leaned to kiss him on the cheek and vowed my commitment to him. Josh then typed, "Ghosts in my room. Can't sleep. I'm scared. Help me." I assured him that I would do everything in my power to help.

In a short while, Josh, his roommate, and the remaining staff filed into the agency van and took off for a community outing, leaving Delores, Carolyn, Amy, and myself alone with the house. Carolyn had brought a camcorder to document the proceedings and capture anything we might miss in real time. She kept the camera running throughout most of the evening. For added protection, all four of us wore crosses or rosaries that had been blessed. Standing in the parking lot, we joined hands as Delores led us in prayer.

We started with the cemetery. As I hadn't previously noticed it, I could now understand how it was overlooked. It was a tiny, narrow plot of land camouflaged in underbrush and relegated to a far corner of the property, across from the long driveway. All told, it couldn't have been larger than fifteen feet square.

In addition to the graveyard's miniscule size, what struck me was its total disarray. Headstones and grave markers seemed to be scattered randomly, many askew, propped against trees, turned in directions opposite from one another, or toppled over completely. They were also packed like sardines, so tight it looked impossible for any caskets to be realistically aligned beneath the numerous, compacted headstones. Then I saw them—three of them together in a row: Edward, Sarah, and Samuel, the names Josh had identified. Something unexpected happened next: I wept for them. I surprised myself to discover that—instead of feeling anger and defiance—I was overcome with love and compassion for them all. It was a pitiful memorial to real people who had lived real lives, some of whom passed before their time. It was like putting a face with a name. A sense of peace and tranquility washed over me; we would be fine and no harm would come to any one of us that night. Once the women had departed the grave-yard, I went back alone and said a prayer for the three for whom I now felt human warmth. We were strangers no longer.

We next walked the outside perimeter of the house. Carolyn kept the camcorder running and photographed all the windows as we passed by. The house was situated on a great, wooded hillside with a gorgeous view of verdant mountain ranges. Immediately we all understood the obvious: this was the original site of the cemetery, not the haphazard sliver of land in which everything was dumped. The house was built over the original graves, of this we felt certain. Standing on the hill, Delores felt that someone was shot or stabbed simultaneous with my reporting a pain in my chest. We came around the other side of the house and noticed a crucifix had been placed on the inside ledge of Josh's bedroom window.

We then entered the house. The yellow paint of the kitchen felt buoyant but Delores and Amy both experienced a choking sensation in their throats and Delores felt pressure on her chest. Delores felt this again when we walked into Josh's bedroom. Then it hit me: some of the deceased had died of tuberculosis, which would've created a closure of the lungs and airway, like being choked. Josh had been grabbing people by the throat. It all crystallized—Josh's actions didn't constitute an act of violent physical aggression, it was a *symbolic communication*. At the height of his anxiety, he was attempting to communicate to others the sensations that had been invisibly impressed upon him, the same sensations that Delores and Amy now experienced and could articulate feeling!

We completed our tour, ending in the basement where I felt it more difficult to breathe and "saw" my nostrils and mouth fill with earth. It was also in the basement that Josh's parents had felt a drastic drop in barometric pressure manifesting in a blast of cold air.

Throughout our survey, we would bounce things off of one another, "Do you feel this?" or "Are you getting anything over here?" At one point, I noticed that the pendulum on a wall clock slowed to a near stop and then picked up momentum after awhile. The clock did not lose time though. Carolyn took the camcorder alone into the spare room, lay still on the bed, and silently fired the lens in the direction of a closet. During this time, the camera malfunctioned; its focus blurred significantly before restoring itself. But this aside, nothing spectacular occurred. We watched Carolyn's video of the entire event twice and noted nothing out of the ordinary. In fact, given the big build up, it was somewhat anticlimactic. What was really going on? Was it authentic? Legitimate? If four highly sensitive people got little to nothing, how was it possible that so much had come undone in our absence?

We wrapped up the evening by returning to Josh's room to again join hands in solemn prayer. Delores acknowledged the presences but asked that they find ways to communicate their needs other than by using Josh. She then suggested that they cross into the glorious white light of the Creator. After saying "Amen," Delores looked at me and asked that I bless the room. "I don't know how," I replied in surprise. "Say what you need to," she calmly directed. I summoned all my thoughts and feelings and prayed that God would protect Josh and keep him safe from harm. I asked the presences to release their hold on Josh, explaining that he was worn thin with exhaustion and that it was unjust and unfair to continue tapping his energy as they had. As I concluded my prayer, I was again weeping profoundly, optimistic that Josh would find relief.

Early the next morning, Amy and I were scheduled to meet back at Laboratory with Josh, his parents, and his staff to review the recommendations I had originally written during his transition to acclimate him in his new home. In the adjustment period, and given everything that had been going on, some things had been overlooked and I wanted to support them all to get back on track.

As we pulled into the driveway, Amy's cell phone rang. It was Delores with important news. After we had parted ways, she and Carolyn went home and played the video for Delores's son (and Josh's staff member) Jerry. At one point when the camera was scanning the house's exterior windows he said, "What was that?" and asked Carolyn to rewind. He had seen a flash of something but wasn't sure exactly what. With the tape rewound, he played it back but *paused it frame by frame* instead of running it at normal speed. There in one of the windows—cloudy-gray and opaque—was a person's face, formed full and complete, it appeared to be that of a bearded man. This was not a reflection; when compared against the static reflection of tree limbs and leaves in the adjacent glass panel, the face image moved and shifted and even seemed to blink.

There had been at least one presence with us the entire time and we never knew it! Did this phantom keep its distance because it knew we were unafraid? Did it maintain a low profile because we were so well protected or because it didn't know what to make of us? One thing rang true for me in that moment—we are all just people, no matter our incarnation. And all people desire to communicate, be heard, and be valued. They were not to be feared, instead they deserved our empathy. The presences in the house may have been dormant or may have always been present since the house was built. They just may not have had the opportunity to communicate through anyone as sensitive as Josh before, and they seized the chance to be heard.

Amy, Delores, and Carolyn would continue to research the property and the deceased families. I would continue to be a resource to Josh and his team, aiding them to empower Josh with the self-advocacy to resist unwanted outside communications. It would be a process that would take some time, sensitivity, and patience.

That morning when I met with Josh, the first thing I did was to ask about his night. He responded by typing, "I slept OK. I love you Bill." I also wrote a story for Josh about his gift similar to those found in this book. After about a month, he was sleeping well every night. He told me, "Story helped me not to be afraid. They will not hurt me. Thank you Bill for understanding." Here is Josh's story:

My Gift

I have a gift.
I am able to see, hear, or feel things others do not.
When this happens, it may be scary or confusing especially if it is unexpected.

I will try to understand myself better.
I will try to understand that I have the power to control my gift.
I will try to think about it like a light switch.
When I am ready to go to sleep, I will turn off the gift like I turn off a light.

If I am awakened by something that may be scary or confusing, I can:
Remind myself to turn it off like a light, or
I can tell what is making me scared or confused to get out and leave me alone, or
I can say a prayer asking God for protection.

I will try to remember that God is always with me and will keep me safe from harm.
I can also find comfort in being with my staff.
I will do my best to try to stay calm and not harm anyone when I am feeling upset.

My staff will remind me to practice turning my gift on and off, especially before going to bed.
I have the power to control my gift.

I was in the right place at the right time, and I thank God that I was involved to the degree of supporting Josh, his parents, and his team members to discern the truth of what was driving his behavior. I am also grateful that Josh had a way of communicating his experience and that those communications were received as his own; otherwise, he was at risk of being unfairly stereotyped, medicated unnecessarily with antipsychotic drugs or, worse yet, physically restrained—all of which could have been aversive and damaging to his own self-image and relationships with the people in his life. This most surely would have led to a downward spiral for Josh instead of a path to upward mobility and self-advocacy. Because Josh's chosen mode of communication is honored, he has begun using spoken language more and more, especially with those in whom he places trust.

The situation was not completely void of humor, though, and there was one synchronous footnote to this eventful trip. Despite Josh's circumstances being extremely serious and intense, my initial visit came with an absurd twist that offered me a whimsical welcome and farewell. On my way into town, the place I usually stop to gas up was full so I drove a bit further down the road to another station. As I was filling my tank, a van pulled up across from me, its business name prominently painted on the side: Ghost Flooring Services. Driving home, I was immersed in thinking of all that had transpired over the past two days and, looking up, passed Spirit Car Wash.

eight

The Ladybug Story

❦

Spiritual symbolism can be found in the most unassuming places and in the least expected ways. Like Jay's rare butterfly from the "Spiritual Protectors" chapter, I discovered that an unpretentious insect could bridge communication gaps—with stunning results—for the parents of one child by saving a relationship and fostering family unity.

Several Novembers ago, I began to notice the appearance of solitary ladybugs in different environments. By the third day (and final appearance of a ladybug), I even liberated one from inside my screened-in porch to the outdoors. Now attuned to such symbolic communications, I decided to investigate further by doing a quick Internet search. On a whim, I typed in "ladybug" and "symbolism," not really expecting there to be much in the way of results. What I quickly discovered was that the ladybug *is* associated with spirituality in Native American shamanism. Because its life is short, the ladybug teaches us to let go of anxieties, *trust* the Great Spirit, and enjoy life. In the course of my ongoing research, the message of trust in God—and myself by extension—was quite direct. My interpretation was that the ladybug's appearance was a message to maintain unwavering faith in a Higher Power.

Further validation came as the week progressed. I received several emails from participants in one of my workshops that were especially generous and complimentary. All were very succinct and in keeping with the "ladybug" message to lighten up and *trust*. Thereafter, and to this day, whenever I feel anxious or stressed more than usual or just need a reminder that I'm on the right path, a single ladybug will manifest to remind me to calm and have faith. Once, in mid-March 2005, I had just completed a day-long autism presentation in Columbus, Ohio, that I concluded by inviting anyone interested to remain afterwards for my autism-and-spirituality discussion. I closed the discussion by telling "The Ladybug Story," and immediately following this, friends who were hosting me noticed *multiple* ladybugs on the chandelier directly outside the auditorium in which we had gathered. However, back when I was first sorting this all out, it would be exactly two weeks until I knew fully the power of the ladybug's symbolism, and its far-reaching application beyond just me.

Thanksgiving week I prepared to travel out of town for several days of monthly consultations accompanied by my local point-of-contact, Craig. Upon arriving, I learned there had been a cancellation for the morning of the last day, with a consultation that same evening. If there's one thing I can't abide, it's waste—especially wasted time. Not wanting to be idle for a day in a very rural area nor stay over an extra night, I asked Craig if he would reschedule the evening group for the empty morning slot or simply postpone until my next trip in mid-January. But rescheduling wasn't possible and the family was in need of meeting this trip, so they said. (Previously, Craig had met briefly with the mother. Given her reports, he suspected that, in addition to the family's daughter, Asperger's Syndrome might have implication for the father as well.) Change doesn't come easily for many people, especially those of us on the autism spectrum. A bit annoyed by the whole situation, I reluctantly acquiesced and before the consultation I resigned to enter into it with the same reverence as any other; anything less would be unprofessional and unworthy. As usual, I prayed before the meeting and asked that the Creator use me for His greater good. In a sly bit of irony, that evening I learned we were headed for a town named Normal.

The trip to the family's home was a good forty-minute drive through winding country back roads under a darkening sky, but it seemed like forever. The longer Craig drove through the middle of nowhere, the more I found myself quietly regretting having consented to come. To top it off, halfway there it started to snow. Hard. Finally we turned down a long, muddy driveway up to an old white farmhouse. Once inside, I relaxed a bit: the house was warm and inviting, courtesy of a roaring blaze in the living room fireplace. I was introduced to two family therapists; Jacob and Rachael, husband and wife; and Amber, the couple's four-year-old daughter and the second of their three children. As I exhaled, the atmosphere became homey and comfortable. A portrait of Christ hung on the wall near some framed family photos.

After settling in, I sat on the nearby piano bench and began the consultation by asking a series of standard questions, which I cautiously transcribed on my yellow ledger.

Within moments of beginning, I noticed a small oval shape alight upon my writing tablet. It was a ladybug. I kept quiet about it, and inconspicuously shooed her away. Thinking myself quite clever, I internally decided that if two more showed up it would most certainly constitute a "sign from God." Sure enough, soon another appeared. Then I felt another on the back of my neck. Then another on my arm, followed by many more! In no time it became apparent that a tiny army of beetles was silently showering down upon me seemingly from out of thin air. The group seated before me sat wide-eyed and open-mouthed; but, as I was already cognizant of the ladybug's symbolism, I found myself intrigued with the synchronicity of it all. I lifted one of the beetles onto my fingertip, momentarily distracted. Embarrassed, Rachael offered a hasty apology that allowed me to affirm for the team what I already knew: "Because the ladybug's life is so short, she teaches us to let go of our frustrations and trust." We completed the remaining questions without further incident, but, inside, my body was humming.

Amber is a physically beautiful child with somber, knowing eyes. As I learned more about Amber, I came to understand her as an old soul, full of wisdom and aptitude well beyond her years. Rachael subsequently wrote:

> When asked her heart's desire Amber responded, "I want to be a princess. Everyone would like me and be nice to me even though I am different. I could make the rules so I don't have to do the things I can't. They would have to do them." At another time when I asked her what she wanted, she replied, "for everyone

to love like Jesus does." She has also communicated
with me that she wants to be involved in music and
art when she gets older. On a daily basis she continues to amaze me with her view of the world and
herself. She has told me on many occasions that I
don't understand her.

These are powerful and stirring observations for a four-
year-old.

Amber communes closely with nature, and collects leaves
from outdoors. At our first meeting, she opened up by telling
me how she nursed her horse, Lucky, after a leg injury, chang-
ing his dressings with painstaking care each morning before
preschool. Rachael then prompted Amber to retrieve a
Polaroid snapshot of her riding Lucky from the refrigerator
where an alphabet magnet held it carefully in place; Amber
dutifully brought the photograph directly to me. In the picture, Amber sits in tight to Lucky as the horse gallops toward
the viewer. However, along the bottom edge of the snapshot
are white, gauzy lights that frame the horse on either side in
spiked starbursts. I asked aloud, "Yes, but what is this?" while
pointing to the white, winged streaks. Rachael offhandedly
explained it away, saying it was a camera flash misfire. They
often had trouble taking good pictures of Amber. Remembering
Kyle's experience in Gettysburg, I told her I'd be very interested
in seeing any others like it at our meeting break.

During the break, I met Rachael in the kitchen as she
flipped through photo albums searching for other examples
to show me. The horse snapshot was on the table and, holding it, I whispered privately, "You do know what this is, don't

you dear?" She paused then cautiously countered, "I know what it is…but *you* tell me." I took a risk. "It's Spirit around her," I confirmed. "Does she have a grandparent that's passed?" Rachael confided that her father had died before Amber was conceived. But before his passing, he told Rachael that she'd know he'd made it to Heaven if her next child was a girl. Now secretly bonded, together we conceded he was most likely a spiritual protector for Amber. Rachael further relinquished her guard and went on to explain that the mysterious white streaks on photos of Amber occurred *regularly*. Even studio portrait photographers refused to sell the family such "defective" photographs, despite being unable to get a clear shot.

I next followed Amber and Rachael upstairs where Amber took pride in showing me her frilly, pink bedroom filled with Barbie dolls. On her wall was another portrait of Jesus that Amber insisted upon maintaining in its precise position. As I looked around, Rachael shared that Amber used to awaken in the middle of the night to entertain the "boy who lived in the attic" with midnight tea parties in her room. Upon checking on her in the morning, Rachael would discover a miniature table set for two. Oddly, Amber told her mother that the "boy" was Rachael's size (Rachael is not a short woman). Intrigued and a bit unnerved, Rachael began to cull ancient history about the house and farm. In her research, Rachael discovered that a man who was intellectually impaired and considered "childlike," had previously lived there. I listened and then expressed concern, wondering if this Spirit knew to release from earthly bounds. Already savvy, Rachael told me they had engaged in a successful releasing process and the early morning tea parties had ceased.

As the meeting wrapped up, the discussion turned from Amber to her father Jacob. Jacob is a tall, husky man with a beautiful, Christ-like visage complete with aquiline nose, gentle blue eyes, and wavy blond hair and beard. He has a special bond with Amber, and their birthdays are a day apart. It seemed that Craig and I had already seen Jacob a year ago in a waiting room. Once Jacob reminded us, I was able to call up the images with certain clarity.

Jacob endured years of self-loathing because of his perceived differences. His struggle brought much stress upon his eighteen-year relationship with Rachael. It had only been three weeks since Rachael uncovered information about Asperger's Syndrome for Amber. In reading it, Jacob finally began to make sense of his own experience. The criterion for Asperger's also applied to him, and he was graciously forthcoming in making this admission. Jacob and I began to share stories, swapping nearly-identical anecdotes about our mutual Asperger's experience. Our kinship was palpable: we found ourselves weeping and smiling and nodding in agreement as our words rang true and parallels emerged. I felt as if Jacob were my twin.

Rachael was now able to courageously admit her own shortcomings in the marriage because of misunderstanding Jacob. It was then that she revealed a bombshell. She had told Jacob she wanted him out after January first. She then planned to file for divorce. *The reason they hadn't separated sooner was because of the scheduled consultation with me.* (Remember, this was the meeting I tried to postpone for another two months!) Rachael now publicly withdrew her ultimatum, and the marriage was saved from imminent termination. I asked that they please support one another during this learning process. Since then, their love has only strengthened.

This meeting was a glorious example of how beautifully the finger of God directs us all to come together, not by chance but by design. Ultimately, Craig and I were drawn to keep the appointment not as much for Amber, but for Jacob. Nor had the ladybug's symbolism of releasing anxieties and learning to trust been for me; it was for this family. I was merely the interpreter. As we parted ways, one of the therapists commented that it was the first time she had ever seen Jacob smile. On the drive home, I silently thanked the Creator for this most perfect example of the ripple effect.

Incidentally, what I learned much later was that, prior to that night, the family had not seen a ladybug in the house for months. Before Amber's bedroom was switched to another room, scads of them used to manifest there and could only be scooped away with a dustpan. Now, it is rare for one or two a year to appear in that room. Also that night, something caught my attention among the typical girly-type pretend play toys and Barbies in Amber's bedroom. There, resting in delicate repose across the headboard of her bed, was a slumbering baby-doll dressed as a ladybug.

nine

Full Circle

❧

The greatest affirmation of all my thinking and personal experience about autism and the God connection came through the gracious courtesy of a group of beautiful, loving persons collectively called the Nightingales. The Nightingales is a monthly gathering of people with various ways of being, many with autism, from across Pennsylvania and its bordering states. Those who don't have a formal autism diagnosis relate well enough to autism to be consulted by researchers and government officials interested in better understanding their experience. Presiding over the Nightingales at the time was my dear friend, Mark.

At present, the Nightingales are a small group, usually no more than a dozen people accompanied by family members or caregivers. But it's an opportunity for folks who have similar experiences to commune with one another.

They all use alternative forms of communication including Facilitated Communication. Each member brings his or her communication device to the meeting, be it a simple paper keyboard or an electronic word processor. Many of the Nightingales do not speak or they may make vocalizations.

Some talk, but like so many, they are better able to most eloquently express themselves in writing. They all have very personal experiences with discrimination and segregation based upon misconceptions. Because they don't speak or communicate fluently they've been stereotyped as unaware and unable to think, decide, and learn.

The Nightingales' literature describes them as people who have varying types of differences that interfere with opportunities to independently pursue most activities that average people take for granted. They are all capable individuals who require varying levels of assistance to engage in the basics of life. Yet they dream, aspire, and hope for a more fulfilling independent life of worth.

They are now involved in setting their own goals and activities as a group. They are committed to the idea of educating speaking people to become more sensitive in their interactions with people who live in silence. They have enjoyed growing respect from professionals, families, and others with differences as spokespersons for those who have been ridiculed, misunderstood, and undereducated.

All of the Nightingales want to be participating members of society. Many are finally taking steps to get on with life by attending regular schools and colleges, gaining and maintaining employment, and making other life decisions. They come together as a group to strengthen their newfound voices, to empower and support themselves and each other, and to wake up the world to the rights of all people to have accessible communication.

The Nightingales began to meet once a month in a location not more than a half hour's drive from my home. I was now in a position to offer my active support to the group. I began attending their meetings and they soon appointed me as their meeting coordinator.

By email, I contacted Mark and asked if he might add to the January 2003 agenda my interest in exploring the topic of autism and spirituality. Being the supreme diplomat, Mark electronically forwarded my request to his email address list, which is many times larger than the number of actual attendees. He received his greatest response ever, and the overwhelming majority indicated strong interest.

On the Sunday of the meeting, the turnout was amazing. There was more than twice the usual number of people, such that we needed to move to a bigger room in the community center where we met.

The meeting began as usual with the Nightingales typing their greetings to one another and discussing bits of business. Their writings were read out loud for all to hear by their accompanying loved ones. Then Mark asked me to discuss my agenda items. I wasn't quite prepared to talk about my current research. I expected to simply gain consensus about the subject as a future meeting topic. But the Nightingales urged me on, saying, "We need to hear from someone who knows our existence," "I long for this," "We know this is our thinking," and "It is real to us." I resigned to share with them all that I had been learning as a result of my renewed spiritual awareness and the wealth of my experiences, including those I've detailed here.

I began by speaking slowly but openly, carefully measuring my words. I talked about my belief that our souls are on an educational journey toward attaining spiritual perfection.

Among the most advanced souls are those who may incarnate as persons with "perceived" severe limitations. There was silence, so I continued. I shared my belief that angels and spiritual protectors closely guarded such individuals. I concluded by discussing the intensity of my recent spiritual development, and I told "The Ladybug Story."

I paused, having finished what I had come there to say. Silence reigned. Then the floodgates opened and the Nightingales began to chime in, one after another, with their stunning validations.

It began as several persons confirmed my position about souls. They stated that I understood them better than most others, and that I spoke truthfully. I was told, "You are a blessing." "Not everyone understands," said another. A young woman responded, "I know people who couldn't handle it also, but that can't keep the truth out of our discussion." Then someone acknowledged, "Cursed with gifts people don't understand, we pretend to be almost normal." One woman agreed, "We are challenged but we are blessed." Another young woman seated to my right was succinct in typing, "I teach loving. I picked my life…I have an old soul that is nearer to Heaven. I was an old soul a long time. I love my life…I want to give my gifts to all."

Others revealed that their spiritual protectors were grandparents with whom they were especially close. "Spirits surround us…they guide and protect us," said Mark. One man asserted that his Grandfather appears to reinforce his purpose in life. "I have seen grandpa so many times when I felt I could not go on. He has told me that I can go on and I should because I have a job to do before I see him again." Another woman said that her grandfather is "always available" and that her spirituality "literally helps me move and live. It helps give me the power to accept what is before me."

The subject of angels brought further validation as some of the Nightingales discussed the number of angels about them or when they appeared to them. One man said, "Angels keep stamping in my path." Another man reflected that an angel "kept me safe once when I was in danger...I am yet not sure if I am liberated by my grandmother or an angel." One young woman said she talks to angels every day.

Many family members were reduced to tears as they learned—for the first time ever—of such divine experiences. Mark wrote that afterwards, he dreamt of me giving roses to all the Nightingales.

The secret of autism was affirmed then and there that Sunday afternoon. The Nightingales' kindly caucus assured me that people with autism are not simply thrust into this world to fend for themselves without some sort of benevolent protection by a means accessible to us all but invisible to most. Not only are people with different ways of being our teachers, here to guide our understanding of compassion, sensitivity, and unconditional love; they may be among our most revered spiritual mentors and valiant visionaries if only we regard them with such deference. At the least, we have much to learn from their patience, forgiveness, resilience, and resourcefulness in how we should all endeavor to interact with one another.

In short order, the Nightingales had so clearly crystallized my research and motivations for compiling this book. I am deeply indebted to them for their candor. They were the absolute counselors in a forum of love, acceptance, and support. They so beautifully endorsed my mission with their wisdom and innate knowledge and confirmed what, for me, had been purely speculative up until that point. I knew then, that if we banded with others who were so demonstratively altruistic, together we had the power to change the world.

And yet despite my exhilaration, I knew I must temper this with the plight of those with autism who deliberately rebuke their spirituality in retaliation of a call unanswered; a failed release from the imprisonment of what they may define as a hopeless or abysmal existence. Clark, fourteen-year-old son of Janet, grapples with finding balance between Asperger's Syndrome, anxiety, and depression. Janet wrote from their Bonita, California home, "Clark has experienced intense pain, emotionally, all his life and cannot reconcile a loving God with his experiences. He once expressed, 'How can there be a God who would make someone like me to suffer so much?'" Given my own history, I could well appreciate Clark's plaintive plea. How *can* we be expected to reconcile our lives when we are working so hard at just *being* instead of *becoming*?

As spiritual practitioner and author Father Thomas Keating has said, "The greatest accomplishment in life is to be who you are, and that means to be who God wanted you to be when He created you." What I trust Clark will eventually come to realize is that, like myself, we each need to figure out how to transcend and make peace within ourselves in our own time. Our suffering is not imposed upon us by our Creator but by the attitudes and mores of others who haven't yet accorded the autistic experience the reverence, appreciation, and

understanding it is due. Perhaps some day soon we will initiate a movement that supports individuals with different ways
of being from a standpoint that shows we've *really* listened.
Wouldn't that be a grand aspiration? The most glorious ripple effect ever.

THE HOMECOMING

Last year, I accepted a friend's invitation to attend a Saturday
evening church service. Although we arrived early, it was
already crowded with parishioners shuffling in, silently seat-
ing themselves, and enacting pensive rituals before Mass. I
could count on one hand the number of times I had been in
such an environment since my childhood days. My friend
understood my desire to remain as inconspicuous as possible
and led us to a discreet pew against the far wall. As the service began, I noticed a number of very young children around
us, all with bright eyes and fresh, open faces. Somewhere, an
archaic cinema projector began to rattle and crank as the
main titles of a faded 8mm home movie flickered before me.

> Mother (in a hushed whisper):
> "I don't know what's wrong with Billy, it's been almost
> ten minutes.
> He just keeps looking over at that same window and
> won't stop crying."
>
> Father (equally hushed):
> "It's getting distracting. Let's just take him out and go."

As the images dissipated from view, I wept at the recollection; my solemn rationale for having cried then still remained a secret. As I cleared my eyes, I looked over at my friend and, then, above to the stained-glass window next to our pew. Stunned, I drew a quick breath and then smiled quietly inside myself: it was the crucifixion—the same scene over which I had once grieved thirty-five years prior. I knew then that I had come home.

JOURNEY'S END

I'd like to conclude *Autism and the God Connection* with a few final thoughts. My gratitude to those who have indulged me thus far. This journey has been a real learning time for me, too. Not surprisingly, when the psychology of it all has vented in my dreams I've sequentially progressed from specific learning environments, transitioning from elementary schools to high school and college campuses. (Lately, I've had my own classroom!)

Melding autism and spirituality may have proven unsettling for some; we all have different comfort levels when it comes to our faith and what we're open to believing. Remember, this is but one prism through which to view the autistic experience, one that may be without personal application. On the other hand, to those already indoctrinated, this all will have been rudimentary—Spiritual Literacy 101. I will be redeemed if this work offers compelling affirmations to those with different ways of being, their families, and caregivers. If you are undecided, simply retain what has made sense and leave the rest behind...you can always come back to it.

Above all, if you take nothing else with you, *please* let it be the concept of presuming intellect and the enactment of the three miracles on a path to opportunity. Through this process, authentic change is truly possible; devoid of this fundamental approach, we risk sowing the seeds that may breed resentment. Myself and other advocates have espoused these positive principles for years now, but it is most gratifying to learn that— even as this book goes to press—the value of respectful, reciprocal relationships with our loved ones who are autistic is now garnering research-based attention from Philadelphia's Temple University, The Center on Intervention for Children and Families at Case Western Reserve University in Cleveland, and The Connections Center for Family and Personal Development in Houston. I anticipate that this research will continue to validate the tenets put forth in this book.

Finally, it is only fitting that a person with autism have the last word in closing this book. Here, then, are the honest, insightful, and profound observations of Michael, a young fifteen-year-old friend and blessed emissary who has always had a deeply spiritual sense of purpose. Michael's heroic and radiant declaration speaks to the true meaning of autism as he envisions it to be.

> I am an Autist. That is the first thing you need to know about me. I am also a messenger from God. All disabled are messengers of God. We are here to help people refind their souls. This is how it works. It is a product of love. When you help a disabled, you do so without expectation of return. It becomes an altruistic act. Altruism is a pure form of love. Love is the key to the soul. God speaks to us through our

souls, but we must be open to the communication. To hear is a wondrous feeling—not words, but emotion. If you want to know the rightness of something, ask yourself how it feels emotionally, not physically. A physical pleasure is just of the world. To feel emotion is eternally based. It is the energy of which we are made.

In coming to this writing, I am sure it is for purpose of learning about autism. It is an honorable goal, and I will try to help you with it. But also understand, it is not God's purpose in having me write this. It is a difficult task to write to both purposes, but I will try. If you come away with a better understanding of your child as an Autist and your child as a Spirit, then I will have succeeded.

Autism is a God-given task; an angelic opportunity for the human soul. For me, it is a blessing and a curse. To be able to speak to God for all your physical life on earth is a true gift. My questions for the reason of things are answered in present, not left waiting for my death. How I am as a person because of my continued connection is a curse and blessing; a blessing to be given the task, a curse to have to actually live it.

Autism is unique to each individual. It is a side effect of the connectedness of soul. Only through a broken body can you retain your spiritual connectedness to the whole.

In the body we lose all memory of our divinity. It is for us to seek experientially in physical form our divineness. The reality is in the physical experience.

Without it there would be just the "knowing" without the experience of "being." "Being" is what life is all about. God gives us the choice of what we want to experience. These choices direct our lives. My choice was to lead people home to their source. It requires my keeping my own connection and that requires a broken body. It is the beauty of it: a whole soul is a broken body; a broken soul is a complete body. To find divinity in a whole body is a very difficult thing. People lose themselves in the physical being and nothing can permeate. All the physical is but an illusion created by the soul yet it controls the soul for its duration on earth. Suffering is God's way of freeing the soul. It is why the greatest goodness is seen there. Goodness always shows itself amid suffering, yet we focus on the bad aspects of it and ignore the beauty of it. Rare is the time that the beauty rises above it. Nine-eleven [September 11, 2001] was such a time.

I am not an Autist by choice. I could have followed my path as any disabled. It is God who chooses how you live out your choice. God loves the act of being and what He is depends on who we are in the physical. When He experiences Himself in His highest form the soul returns to the whole. Before that can be possible, God has to evolve in each of us. It takes many lives to reach a physical practice of God's love…How all come to be a God, how all come to rejoin God, how all come to benefit God is in bringing Him the sensation of being. He gets to see and experience His Godliness through us.

appendix A

Bibliography

⚬

In writing *Autism and the God Connection*, I supplemented the accounts of my own experiences, and those of others, with supporting information drawn from the following published sources.

Altea, Rosemary. *Proud Spirit: Lessons, Insights, and Healing from "The Voice of the Spirit World."* New York: William Morrow and Company, Inc., 1997.

Anderson, George. *Lessons from the Light: Extraordinary Messages of Comfort and Hope from the Other Side.* New York: G. P. Putnam's Sons, 1999.

Aron, Elaine N. *The Highly Sensitive Person: How to Thrive When the World Overwhelms You.* Secaucus, New Jersey: Carol Publishing Group, 1996.

"Autistic Children Benefit Greatly from Relationship Development Intervention Program." *Medical News Today.* April 20, 2005.

Ball, Marshall. *Kiss of God: The Wisdom of a Silent Child.*
Deerfield Beach, Florida: Health Communications, Inc.,
1999.

Batchelor, Doug. *To See the King: Seven Steps to Salvation.*
Sacramento, CA: Mountain Ministry, 2001.

Bodine, Echo. *The Gift.* Novato, CA: New World Library,
2003.

Bolton, Patrick F., Rebecca J. Park, J. Nicholas P. Higgins,
Paul D. Griffiths, and Andrew Pickles. "Neuro-epileptic
Determinants of Autism Spectrum Disorders in
Tuberous Sclerosis Complex." *Brain* 125, no. 6 (June
2002): 1247–1255.

Brazier, David. *The New Buddhism.* New York: Palgrave,
2002.

Brinkley, Dannion. *At Peace in the Light: The Further
Adventures of a Reluctant Psychic Who Reveals the Secret of
Your Spiritual Powers.* New York: HarperCollins, 1995.

Brinkley, Dannion, and Paul Perry. *Saved by the Light: The
True Story of a Man Who Died Twice and the Profound
Revelations He Received.* New York: Villard Books, 1994.

Brown, Chester D., Jr. M.A. "American Indians with
Disabilities and Spirituality." *Wellness News,* New Mexico
Office of Disability and Health, Summer 2001.

Browne, Sylvia. *Blessings from the Other Side: Wisdom and Comfort from the Afterlife for this Life*. New York: Dutton, 2000.

———. *Conversations with the Other Side*. Carlsbad, CA: Hay House, 2002.

———. *Life on the Other Side: A Psychic's Tour of the Afterlife*. New York: Dutton, 2000.

———. *The Nature of Good and Evil*. Carlsbad, CA: Hay House, 2001.

———. *The Other Side and Back: A Psychic's Guide to Our World and Beyond*. New York: Dutton, 1999.

———. *Past Lives, Future Healing: A Psychic Reveals the Secrets of Good Health and Great Relationships*. New York: Dutton, 2001.

———. *Sylvia Browne's Book of Angels*. Carlsbad, CA: Hay House, 2003.

———. *Sylvia Browne's Book of Dreams*. New York: Dutton, 2002.

———. *Visits from the Afterlife: The Truth about Hauntings, Spirits, and Reunions with Lost Loved Ones*. New York: Dutton, 2003.

Brussat, Frederic, and Mary Ann Brussat. *Spiritual Literacy: Reading the Sacred in Everyday Life*. New York: Scribner, 1996.

Burnham, Sophy. *A Book of Angels: Reflections on Angels Past and Present and True Stories of How They Touch Our Lives*. New York: Ballantine Books, 1990.

Byrd, Charles W. *To Fly with the Angels: Spiritual Messages Received by Mary Nell*. Xlibris Corporation, 2000.

Calaprice, Alice. *The Quotable Einstein*. Princeton University Press, 1996.

Cardinal, D.N., Hanson, D., and Wakeham, J. "Investigation of Authorship in Facilitated Communication." *Mental Retardation* 34, no. 4 (August 1996): 231–42.

Chopra, Deepak. *How to Know God: The Soul's Journey into the Mystery of Mysteries*. New York: Harmony Books, 2000.

Colmanares, Clinton. "Multiple Genetic 'Flavors' May Explain Autism." *Medical News Today*, July 25, 2005.

Cook, Jr., Edwin H., and Bennett L. Leventhal. "The Serotonin System in Autism." *Current Opinion in Pediatrics*, August 1996.

Cranston, Sylvia, and Carey Williams. *Reincarnation: A New Horizon in Science, Religion, and Society*. New York:

Crown Publishers, 1984.

Dyer, Wayne. *Ten Secrets for Success and Inner Peace.* Carlsbad, CA: Hay House, 2001.

Edelson, Ed. "Science Points to a 'Sixth Sense.'" *HealthDay News,* February 17, 2005.

Edward, John. *Crossing Over: The Stories behind the Stories.* San Diego, CA: Jodere Group, 2001.

———. *One Last Time.* New York: Berkeley Publishing Group, 1998.

———. *After Life: Answers from the Other Side.* Carlsbad, CA: Hay House, 2003.

Fenimore, Angie. *Beyond the Darkness: My Near Death Journey to the Edge of Hell and Back.* New York: Bantam Books, 1995.

Foster, Andrew. "Loving People is Loving God: An Autistic Man Talks about Spirituality." *The Presbyterian Record* (The National Magazine of the Presbyterian Church in Canada), May 2005.

Fox, Matthew, and Rupert Sheldrake. *The Physics of Angels: Exploring the Realm Where Science and Spirit Meet.* San Francisco, CA: HarperSanFrancisco, 1996.

Freud, Sigmund (Translated by Dr. A.A. Brill). *The Interpretation of Dreams*. New York: Random House, 1978 (original publication date: 1900).

Gage, Dan, and Gage, Toni. "Autism: Declaring War." *The Autism Perspective* 1, no. 3 (Summer 2005).

Goldman, Karen. *Angel Encounters: True Stories of Divine Intervention*. New York: Simon & Schuster, 1995.

Grandin, Temple, and Catherine Johnson. *Animals in Translation: Using the Mysteries of Autism to Decode Animal Behavior*. New York: Scribner, 2005.

Hamer, Dean. *The God Gene: How Faith is Hardwired into Our Genes*. New York: Doubleday, 2004.

Holliday Willey, Liane. *Pretending to be Normal: Living with Asperger's Syndrome*. London: Jessica Kingsley Publishers, Ltd., 1999.

Holy Bible, Old and New Testaments (King James Version).

"Is God an Anti-Depressant? Studies Show That Religious People Are Happier." ABC News Internet Ventures, January 24, 2005.

John Paul II, Pope. *Crossing the Threshold of Hope*. New York: Alfred A. Knopf, 1994.

Katz, Illana. "Does Autism Offer Special Gifts?" *The Jewish Journal of Greater Los Angeles*, May 27, 2005.

Kephart, Beth. *A Slant of Sun: One Child's Courage*. New York: W.W. Norton & Company, Inc., 1998.

Kluger, Jeffrey. "Is God in Our Genes?" *Time*, October 25, 2004.

MacGregor, Hilary E. "Far-off Healing." *Los Angeles Times*, May 2, 2005.

Mandelbaum, Yitta Halberstam. *Small Miracles: Extraordinary Coincidences from Everyday Life*. Holbrook, MA: Adams Media Corp., 1997.

Mark, Barbara. *Angelspeake*. New York: Simon & Schuster, 1995.

Millman, Dan, and Doug Childers. *Divine Interventions: True Stories of Mystery and Miracles That Change Lives*. Emmaus, Pennsylvania: Daybreak Books, 1999.

Moody, Raymond. *Reunions: Visionary Encounters with Departed Loved Ones*. New York: Villard Books, 1993.

———. *Coming Back: A Psychiatrist Explores Past Life Journeys*. New York: Bantam Books, 1990.

————. *Life After Life: The Investigation of a Phenomenon—Survival of Bodily Death*. New York: Bantam Books, 1975.

————. *The Light Beyond*. New York: Bantam Books, 1988.

Moore, Thomas. *Care of the Soul: Cultivating Depth and Sacredness in Everyday Life*. New York: HarperCollins, 1992.

Mulder, Erik J M.D., George M Anderson, PhD, Ido P Kema, PhD, Annelies de Bildt, PhD, Natasja DJ van Lang, PhD et al. "Platelet Serotonin Levels in Pervasive Developmental Disorders and Mental Retardation: Diagnostic Group Differences, Within-Group Distribution, and Behavioral Correlates" *Journal of the American Academy of Child and Adolescent Psychiatry* 43, no. 4 (April 2004).

Newton, Michael, Ph.D. *Journey of Souls: Case Studies of Life between Lives*. St. Paul, Minnesota: Llewellyn Publications, 1994.

————. *Destiny of Souls: New Case Studies of Life between Lives*. St. Paul, Minnesota: Llewellyn Publications, 2000.

Norton, Amy. "Low-Cost Therapy Shows Promise for Autism." *Journal of Developmental and Behavioral Pediatrics*, April 2005.

O'Neill, Jasmine Lee. *Through the Eyes of Aliens: A Book about Autistic People*. London: Jessica Kingsley Publishers, Ltd., 1999.

Olmstead, Dan. "The Age of Autism: But What about 1930?" UPI Consumer Health News, August 8, 2005.

Omotosho, Philip. "A Review of Current Thoughts on Localized Structural Lesions in Autistic Disorder." *The Child Advocate Autism and Neurology Page*, 2002–2003.

Orloff, Judith. *Second Sight*. New York: Warner Books, 1996.

Pearsall, Paul. *Making Miracles*. New York: Prentice Hall Press, 1991.

Pentzell, Nick. "Fools of God." *The Other Side: Strength for the Journey* 40, no. 2 (March–April 2004).

Redfield, James. *The Celestine Prophecy*. New York: Warner Books, 1993.

"Researchers Observe Abnormalities in Brains of Autism Patients." American Academy of Neurology news release, February, 13, 2002.

Saylor, Frederica. "Brain Chemicals Key to Spiritual Experience." *Science and Theology News*, March 2004.

Schwartz, Gary. *The Afterlife Experiments: Breakthrough Scientific Evidence of Life After Death*. New York: Pocket Books, 2002.

Schworm, Peter. "Their Leap of Faith: Developmentally Disabled Children Learn of Religion." *The Boston Globe*, January 31, 2005.

Semple, Ian. "God Under a Microscope." *Sydney Morning Herald*, March 2, 2005.

Shroder, Tom. *Old Souls: The Scientific Evidence for Past Lives*. New York: Simon and Schuster, 1999.

Sparrow, Gregory Scott. *I Am with You Always: True Stories of Encounters with Jesus*. New York: Bantam Books, 1995.

Stillman, William. *Demystifying the Autistic Experience: A Humanistic Introduction for Parents, Caregivers, and Educators*. London: Jessica Kingsley Publishers, Ltd., 2002.

Sutcliffe, James S., Ryan J. Delahanty, and Harish C. Prasad et al. "Allelic Heterogeneity at the Serotonin Transporter Locus (*SLC6A4*) Confers Susceptibility to Autism and Rigid-Compulsive Behaviors." *The American Journal of Human Genetics* 77, no. 2 (August 2005).

Teasdale, Wayne. *The Mystic Heart: Discovering a Universal Spirituality in the World's Religions*. Novato, California: New World Library, 1999.

Teresa, Mother. *The Joy in Loving: A Guide to Daily Living with Mother Teresa*. New York: Viking Press, 1996.

———. *The Love of Christ: Spiritual Counsels*. New York: Harper & Row, 1982.

Theisen, Donna, and Dary Matera. *Childlight: How Children Reach out to Their Parents from the Beyond*. Far Hills, New Jersey: New Horizon Press, 2001.

Tolle, Eckhart. *The Power of Now: A Guide to Spiritual Enlightenment*. Novato, CA: New World Library, 1999.

Van Praagh, James. *Healing Grief: Reclaiming Life after any Loss*. New York: Dutton, 2000.

———. *Heaven and Earth: Making the Psychic Connection*. New York: Simon & Schuster, 2001.

———. *Reaching to Heaven: A Spiritual Journey through Life and Death*. New York: Dutton, 1999.

———. *Talking to Heaven: A Medium's Message of Life after Death*. New York: Dutton, 1997.

Walsch, Neal Donald. *Conversations with God: An Uncommon Dialogue*. New York: G.P. Putnam's Sons, 1995.

Wester Anderson, Joan. *Where Angels Walk: True Stories of Heavenly Visitors.* New York: Ballantine Books, 1992.

Williamson, Marianne. *Everyday Grace: Having Hope, Finding Forgiveness, and Making Miracles.* New York: Riverhead Books, 2002.

Zukav, Gary. *The Heart of the Soul: Emotional Awareness.* New York: Simon & Schuster, 2002.

———. *The Seat of the Soul.* New York: Simon & Schuster, 1989.

———. *Soul Stories.* New York: Fireside, 2000.

Additional Resources

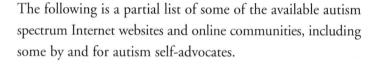

The following is a partial list of some of the available autism spectrum Internet websites and online communities, including some by and for autism self-advocates.

Advisory Board on Autism & Related Disorders (ABOARD). *www.aboard.org*

ASCEND Group. An Asperger's Syndrome alliance for the Greater Philadelphia region. *www.ascendgroup.org*

Asperger's Association of New England. Fosters awareness, respect, acceptance, and support for people with Asperger's and their families. *www.aane.org*

Asperger Syndrome Education Network, Inc. Headquartered in New Jersey. *www.aspennj.org*

Aspies for Freedom. A safe and comfortable forum for Aspies and those with autism. *www.aspiesforfreedom.com*

Autism/Asperger's Digest Magazine. *www.autismdigest.com*

Autism Living and Working. Pennsylvania-based group of parents and others who support community living and housing for folks with autism. *www.autismlivingworking.org*

Autism National Committee. *www.autcom.org*

Autism Network International. An autistic-run self-help and advocacy organization for people on the autism spectrum. *www.ani.ac*

Autism One Radio. Online radio programming established by parents. *www.autismone.org/radio*

The Autism Perspective (TAP). Website for the magazine *The Autism Perspective. www.theautismperspective.org*

The Autism Service Center. A national autism hotline and website. *www.autismservicescenter.org*

Autism Society of America. *www.autism-society.org*

Autism Spectrum Quarterly. Autism "magajournal" with articles by, for, and about individuals with autism. *www.ASQuarterly.com*

Autism Talk. An online community with a variety of discussion categories on all aspects of autism. *www.autismtalk.net*

Autism Today. Latest news and resources for autism and autism-related issues. *www.autismtoday.com*

Autistics.Org. Resources by and for persons on the autism spectrum, including many links to other self-advocates' websites. *www.autistics.org*

The Bubel/Aiken Foundation. *www.thebubelaikenfoundation.org*

Chat Autism. A chat and community forum for those with autism and their families. *www.chatautism.com*

Cure Autism Now. *www.cureautismnow.org*

The Dan Marino Foundation. *www.danmarinofoundation.org*

Donna Williams, prominent autism self-advocate and author. *www.donnawilliams.net*

The Doug Flutie Jr. Foundation for Autism, Inc. *www.dougflutiejrfoundation.org*

Families for Early Autism Treatment. *www.feat.org*

The Global and Regional Asperger Syndrome Partnership (GRASP). An informational, educational, and advocacy organization operated by persons on the autism spectrum. *www.grasp.org*

The Gray Center, website of educator and social stories founder, Carol Gray. *www.thegraycenter.org*

Lianne Holliday Willey, Asperger's Syndrome self-advocate and author. *www.aspie.com*

Looking Up, the monthly international autism newsletter. *www.lookingupautism.org*

MAAP Services. Covers autism, Asperger's syndrome, and Pervasive Developmental Disorder. *www.maapservices.org*

National Alliance for Autism Research. *www.naar.org*

National Association of Councils on Developmental Disabilities. *www.nacdd.org*

National Parent to Parent Network website. *www.P2PUSA.org*

Networks for Training and Development. Pennsylvania-based training and resource organization for caregivers of people with differences, including autism, that supports the use of Augmentative and Alternative Communication methods. *www.networksfortraining.org*

Neurodiversity.com. A demagogic collection of information "honoring the variety of human wiring" that also includes national news reports on the abuses committed against persons with autism. *www.neurodiversity.com*

Online Asperger's Syndrome Information and Support (OASIS). Website created by parents. *www.aspergersyndrome.org*

Ontario Adult Autism Research and Support Network (OAARSN). *www.ont-autism.uoguelph.ca*

Stephen Shore, Asperger's Syndrome self-advocate, consultant, and author. *www.autismasperger.net*

Spectrum Publications. Home of *Spectrum* magazine. *www.spectrumpublications.com*

Temple Grandin, perhaps the best known autism self-advocate and bestselling author. *www.templegrandin.com*

Tony Attwood, acknowledged Asperger's Syndrome authority. *www.tonyattwood.com*

Unlocking Autism. Website with a listserv to connect parents, teens, and adults with autism and Asperger's. *www.unlockingautism.org*

AUGMENTATIVE AND ALTERNATIVE COMMUNICATION

The following Internet websites and online communities support the use of Augmentative and Alternative Communication, including Facilitated Communication, as a viable and valid alternative to speech for individuals unable to talk or those who cannot speak clearly.

Autism National Committee Position on Facilitated Communication. *www.autcom.org/facilitated.html*

Autism Society of Wisconsin Resolution on Facilitated Communication.
www.geocities.com/athens/forum/8925/resolut1.htm

Breaking the Barriers. A website supported by TASH (an international organization for persons with disabilities and their supporters) that includes vision statements, a call to action, and personal stories. *www.breaking-the-barriers.org*

Communication and Learning Enterprises (CandLE). An organization devoted to developing the use of Facilitated Communication Training in the United Kingdom for children and adults with speech and motor impairment. *www.contactcandle.co.uk*

DEAL (Dignity, Education, and Language) Communication Centre, Australia, Rosemary Crossley, PhD, Director. *http://home.vicnet.net.au/~dealcc/*

FC Net. Ashland University, Ohio-based website serving a global, open distribution list of persons interested in all aspects of Facilitated Communication.
www.geocities.com/athens/forum/8925/fc_net.htm

FC World. An international Internet group of Facilitated Communication users, their educators, and caregivers.
http://groups.yahoo.com/group/FCworld/

Facilitated Communication Coalition of Indiana.
www.bloomington.in.us/~fcindy//

Facilitated Communication Institute, Syracuse University,
New York, Dr. Douglas Biklen, Director.
http://soeweb.syr.edu/thefci

Facilitated Communication Resource Directory. A national
and international resource list of individuals who have
been designated as FC points of contact in their countries
or states. *http://soeweb.syr.edu/thefci/7-4ric.htm*

Facilitated Communication in Washington. Washington
state's Facilitated Communication website.
www.geocities.com/athens/forum/8925/home.html

Michigan Protection and Advocacy Service Model Policy on
Facilitated Communication.
http://soeweb.syr.edu/thefci/guide-mi.htm

The Pennsylvania Perspective: Implementation of Best
Practice in Facilitated Communication Training.
http://soeweb.syr.edu/thefci/guide-pa.htm

State of New Hampshire Department of Health and
Human Services Division of Developmental Services
Guidelines for the Use of Facilitated Communication.
http://soeweb.syr.edu/thefci/8-3new.htm

TASH Resolution on Facilitated Communication.
www.tash.org/resolutions/res02faccom.htm

The University of Maine Center for Community Inclusion
and Disability Studies. *www.umaine.edu/cci/*

Vermont Facilitated Communication Network.
www.uvm.edu/~uapvt/faccom.html

Watch Our Words. An organization for users of Facilitated
Communication and their friends in Colorado.
http://donna.jdowning.com/index.htm

About the Author

❧

Photo © Tim McGowan

William Stillman is the author of *Demystifying the Autistic Experience: A Humanistic Introduction for Parents, Caregivers, and Educators*, which has been highly praised by the autism self-advocacy community. His other titles include *The Everything Parent's Guide to Children with Asperger's Syndrome: Help, Hope, and Guidance* and *The Everything Parent's Guide to Children with Bipolar Disorder: Professional, Reassuring Advice to Help You Understand and Cope*. Stillman also writes a column, "Through the Looking Glass," for the national quarterly magazine *The Autism Perspective* and is on the publication's advisory board.

As an adult with Asperger's Syndrome, a mild "cousin" of autism, Stillman's message of reverence and respect has touched thousands through his acclaimed autism workshops and private consultations. His national television appearances include *CNN Medical News* and the *Maury Povich Show*.

Stillman has a BS in Education from Millersville University in Pennsylvania, and has worked to support people with different ways of being since 1987. He was formerly the Pennsylvania Department of Public Welfare, Office of Mental Retardation's statewide point person for children with intellectual impairment, mental health issues, and autism.

Stillman is at the forefront of the autism self-advocacy movement and is founder of the Pennsylvania Autism Self-Advocacy Coalition, which endeavors to educate and advise state and local government, law enforcement, educators, and the medical community. He serves on Pennsylvania's Autism Task Force and is on several autism and Asperger's advisory boards including the Youth Advocate Programs' National Autism Advisory Committee. Stillman has collaborated with Temple University to develop a relationship-based curriculum for Youth Advocate Programs which will set the national standard by which mental health workers will be trained to support children and adolescents with autism. He is also the coordinator for a Pennsylvania-based meeting group of individuals who use Augmentative and Alternative Communication.

Stillman is coauthor of several successful books about his life-long passion, *The Wizard of Oz*. His website address is www.williamstillman.com.